FUTURE WOMEN

Y FEMALE ENTREPRENEURSHIP AND THE
INDUSTRIAL REVOLUTION IN THE ERA OF
OCKCHAIN AND CRYPTOCURRENCY

Y CHRISSA MCFARLANE,
ER AND CEO OF PATIENTORY

FUTURE WOMEN: Minority Female Entrepreneurship and the Fourth Industrial Revolution in the Era of Blockchain and Cryptocurrency

TABLE OF CONTENTS

DEDICATION

"But if women aren't put in the spotlight, that's where you have an issue of future people—people who are not in the community already but are maybe thinking about it—feeling, like we talked about, not welcomed. That's exactly what we experience in tech. And then when finally women start to join then they feel like they need to leave, and they don't stay on. And I would be scared of a future there."

—Veronica Reynolds, Founder Blockchain UCLA

This is dedicated to Future Women everywhere,
rising up every day to take their place at the table.

The time has come.

To Sonia and Collin

INTRO

"The stakes are huge... The early winners in these spaces set the tone and start a cascade of effects that last for the entire generation of the space. They become the investors. They become the social community leaders. It matters a lot. I think a lot of people are feeling like they don't want history to repeat itself. They don't want the same thing that we saw with the last startup boom to happen again."

—Nellie Bowles, *The New York Times*

The steam engine, the age of science and mass production, and now the rise of digital technology joined by blockchain and cryptocurrency lead us into the Fourth Industrial Revolution with one difference—the rise of minority women entrepreneurship. But, it won't be easy. We minority women have to lift each other up and share what we know so we can work together as a force in business to allow us to change the world in ways it has never seen before.

Seem too hard to tackle? Try living as a minority female entrepreneur in a world where a boys' club holds all the keys.

Got your attention? Good. Because this is my passion. I want to create more successful minority female entrepreneurs today. I want you to know that the world needs you. Business needs you. But, do you know why?

Much has been written about female empowerment to address the reasons why we minority women need to discover our passion and live to our full potential. All of us are certainly aware that we collectively make society a better place when we use our God-given gifts to the fullest. While this book is, in part, about my own empowerment journey, it's also so much more. This book is about inclusivity and exposing my vulnerabilities so that any minority woman thinking about diving into this field has a real look at what the process was like for me with the hopes that you, the reader, will be inspired to do your own thing and achieve great success in the field of your expertise.

I believe that when the needs and considerations of one segment of a community aren't addressed or are marginalized, everyone ends up leaving money on the table. So get ready to launch your frustrations out the window, and plug into the Fourth Industrial Revolution of female minority entrepreneurship.

You are a Future Woman.

What? I'll never find a seat at that table, you say?

There was a time when I couldn't imagine myself at that table either. But don't worry; by the end of this book, you'll have a roadmap so you can avoid some of the common roadblocks on the journey to making your entrepreneurial dreams come true along with some tips to help get there faster than I did. When you look at the statistics, you know we have an uphill climb.

"The number of black women entrepreneurs is doubling each year, but the percentage of venture capital raised is practically non-existent. Of the $424.7 billion of funding raised since 2009, only $289 million went to black women."[1]

When it came time for me to try and take my seat, I was politely shooed

---

[1] https://www.businessinsider.com/mahmee-founder-calls-on-silicon-valley-investors-to-be-more-courageous-2019-2

away. Venture Capitalists (VCs) attended my meetings, but nothing would ever come from them. The experience gave me the feeling that while I had the right to dream the biggest dreams in the world, there would be no way to make them a reality.

As it turned out, though, I had bigger problems. See, I wanted to create an industry that didn't even exist yet—using blockchain and cryptocurrency to help the worldwide healthcare industry service patients in ways that would make every medical record easily accessible by healthcare providers. To do that, I had to create what amounts to a new language and teach that language to potential investors before they could properly fund or even spread the word about my company.

You try explaining to people that investments can be tokenized and connected by blockchain one day in order to create a patient-centered protocol supported by blockchain technology to change the way healthcare stakeholders manage electronic medical data and interact with clinical care teams. Talk about an uphill climb! Some days, opening up a lemonade stand on the beach seemed like a better option.

I remember one day, long before I'd even dreamt of Patientory, when I'd similarly had the rug pulled out from under me. In 2015, on a beautiful day in May, I ended up walking into St. Patrick's Cathedral eight blocks away from 42nd street in Midtown, the heart of New York City. As soon as I walked into the gothic building, I breathed in the scent of holy incense and felt the church's ominous, eerie presence.

I scanned people sitting in the church pews—all types and races of people, from a migrant Mexican construction worker to an elderly white woman on her lunch break, to typical tourists. Wafts of smoke filled a construction zone at the church's entrance where the narthex had been lined with burning candles left by hundreds of people who'd already prayed and cast their cares and burdens in the flames. I remembered lighting candles with my mother and father at an early age at a Catholic church, although they ended up raising my sisters and I in the Pentecostal church. Their walk of faith informed my own and led me there on that difficult day.

Like the family next to me, I donated and retrieved a new white candle. I lit it in the flame of a burning candle and watched their flames combine before my eyes. Then I placed my candle in a bronze, wax-encrusted holder where it sat adding its light to the ribbons of flickering light of the other candles illuminating the church. In the soft golden glow, I put my hands together and bowed my head. I had just been fired that morning.

"Dear God, please grant me clarity and grace as I move forward in my journey. Amen."

Like many recent grads, we enter the real world with high hopes and expectations, thinking we're ready to take over the world. Never in a million years did I expect to be fired. It had been six years after my graduation. I had also never expected to be working in a field different than the one I'd hoped to carve out for myself as a little girl. As I sat there watching my flame, now burning with my hopes for clarity and grace, my professional life sort of passed in front of me. I started to get indignant, which didn't feel that good while kneeling in prayer. See, it seemed I'd done everything "right" during the rite of passage known as college. On this day, as I bowed my head into my folded hands still in prayer, a part of me already felt as if I'd failed.

As I sat there in the church, I reflected on what I'd considered other failures in my life, like how my childhood dream of becoming a physician had been compromised. But I didn't know then as I stared at the flames that God would answer my prayer. He granted me the clarity and grace I needed to persevere. His provision helped me to stumble across a true gem of an experience that would try me in ways I could never have imagined and also helped me dig deeper inside where I found myself and my true calling.

I hope my entrepreneurial journey and the profiles written within these pages help to inspire your journey as a Future Woman. If you're on the road to becoming a Future Woman, at times, you'll meet resistance, sometimes massive resistance. My dream is that the ideas in this book can serve as a roadmap to help you avoid some of the pitfalls and roadblocks I encountered and help you meet that resistance with grace and confidence. When you're in the heat of challenges that will occur, I hope you'll come back here to not only find comfort from women who've gone through similar experiences, but use the stories of the other Future Women profiled here as a resource to unlock your entrepreneurial dream. I also hope by reading this book you'll be empowered to take the next step so that your ideas are not only actionable but also profitable. Here's to your great success!

MY ENTREPRENEURSHIP

The core issue was why, as a patient, do I not have access to my entire health data?"

—Chrissa McFarlane

Somehow, three months before I heard the words *we are letting you go*, I'd experienced a disconnect between the place and the work I inhabited. I'd morphed into something I wasn't and it felt like the powers that be had forced me to fit in an uncomfortable box that definitely didn't feel like a place where I belonged. From the rudeness of a constantly competitive colleague to whispers around the office, the culture had diminished to the point of becoming toxic due to issues with leadership, the people whom I thought would protect me.

In the aftermath, I processed the failed leadership issues we'd faced at the startup, many typical dysfunctions of a team that Patrick Lencioni outlines in his book *The Five Dysfunctions of a Team*—from the office politics, to relationships—you name it! The book was recommended reading by an executive coach who was brought in to enhance culture at that startup. This process caused me to look at the healthcare industry, overall. And one thing became clear—I needed to go out on my own to accomplish my heart's desire. Not that I thought I'd ever start my own business so soon, but, in hindsight, I believe the loathsome experience I had at the startup planted the seed for me to start my own company. At that point, I began to formulate what I felt was a solid solution to tackle the difficulties faced by the healthcare industry and thereby transform a negative experience into a positive one.

Now, my team and I are on a mission to make healthcare more personal. By this, I mean creating a mindset to empower businesses and individuals with the tools to achieve improved health outcomes. My company provides the necessary app that can collect all the consumers' health and personal data—from medical records to how many calories eaten in a day, how many hours slept, and even mindfulness data like meditation hours. Then, we give an overall score, which is provided on our dashboard so the consumer can easily assess if they're meeting their targeted goals for an improved lifestyle.

In this way, a plan is created and in place that can be implemented easily in busy, everyday lives. I would say that our app provides a definitive daily treatment plan for how to maximize or improve personal health outcomes. But beyond that, we also give people a way to share data with doctors and hospitals seamlessly so that doctors are able to provide the best possible individualized care to their patients. Basically, our goal is to make consumers the masters of their well-being and health information while alleviating healthcare professionals from the time-consuming burden of paperwork and online data processing."

What do I mean by this? Basically, the trend in healthcare today is one in which doctors are in servitude to data that arose in the aftermath of the Health Insurance Portability and Accountability Act (HIPAA). While privacy laws are in place for good reasons, such as the protection of confidential information, the regulations around implementation has set up an undue burden on healthcare institutions to manage this confidential data, which sets up reams of paperwork that need to be processed and results in many barriers to sharing information.

I knew something had to change after seeing these complications arise firsthand from my early introduction to the healthcare industry as a high school student, shadowing provider specialists around New York City.

I founded Patientory from both personal and professional experiences and frustration with patients not being able to have a central depository of their own health information, as well as the ability to access support from a community. Our core purpose in making healthcare personal is to empower patients globally by giving them access to their health information and connecting them with their many caregivers for improved health outcomes and well-being. Essentially, we're not only saving the healthcare industry a lot of money but also showing our customers how to decrease capital expenditures and penalties by improving operational security and adherence.

In the following chapters, I'll elaborate a bit more on the challenges that I met on the road to this successful token sale and Series A round of funding. But before we get started, I'll reflect on a few of the biggest challenges I faced as an entrepreneur so you can understand what will unfold in the rest of the book.

The biggest challenge in my job as an entrepreneur who has built an industry from scratch wasn't the development of the blockchain protocols or even trying to articulate this new industry to visionaries who could invest and get on board to help make the company a reality. Rather, my biggest challenge became the awareness I would need to cultivate and develop the abilities I had to acquire to effectively choose and mentor the right team. The next challenge I faced involved overcoming an unexpected surprise forcing me to go outside of the traditional venture capitalist system to get people to accept a shared vision of my company.

In my opinion, the key to the success of any entrepreneur lies in finding enlightened people who are as equally invested as the founder in helping move the business forward. Sometimes, this was difficult for me, but it didn't stop me from moving forward. Getting the right team together has taught me a lot about leadership. In the following chapters, I expand on Future Woman mindsets that can help make your entrepreneurial dreams a reality.

I've organized the chapters to have titles that outline the characteristics I believe are needed in order to become a Future Woman, a minority woman entrepreneur in a world that only gave 0.0006% of the 424.7 billion dollars invested in founders between 2009 and 2017 to Black women.[2] Sure, I could have given up when I reached out to over 500 VCs for funding when they all said no. But I simply made the choice to find another way.

And when I did, I discovered much needed support in an ecosystem of mentors and cohorts who had my back. An ecosystem is definitely one of the most important things for the survival of startups and the female minority entrepreneur. In order for my startup to grow, the ecosystem has provided the resources and opportunities I needed to keep me on track. That meant access, like invitations to events that enabled me to connect with people, or resources to help expand different aspects of the business, marketing know-how to help grow the company, financial expertise to help smooth out day-to-day operations, or just validation about my business plan with business coaching and support. My startup needed these important resources to thrive. Through it all, I discovered that my biggest entrepreneurial disappointments turned out to be my biggest blessings, and I also found that my success lay in

---

[2] https://projectdiane.digitalundivided.com

my capacity to overcome failure—what I believe is at the heart of the mindset of Future Women.

CRYPTOCURRENCY AND BLOCKCHAIN DEMYSTIFIED

*"Healthcare is the third largest spend in our economy, in terms of GDP. Based on my past experiences working in digital healthcare startups and telemedicine, I looked at the main problem we face in healthcare—**not having empowered patients and not having patient engagement in the healthcare system.***

In my eyes, healthcare had really been run by the payers and those dishing out reimbursements for medical care. I decided that one of the biggest problems was also these electronic medical records that came into being over the past 10 to 15 years.

*But they just sat there, essentially and were just basically banks of health data. **They didn't want to share it with anyone.***

So to me, the core issue was why, as a patient, do I not have access to my health data? Why am I having to request a fax in the year 2014 and 2015 for my healthcare data?"

—Chrissa McFarlane

Blockchain, the magic book

When I first began speaking on panels to different audiences about blockchain, I heard an interesting, powerful analogy. Another panelist asked the audience to think of the concept of blockchain as a magical book. In order to survive on earth, over 7 billion people have a copy of this magical book, but you only have access to the pages that relate to your life in that book. As you continue to create more experiences and life journeys, your part of the book gets written and updated.

You share your chapters with other people by giving them public access keys to your pages within the book so you can transfer your experiences with other people. Everyone has the same book and everyone's stories are being updated every five minutes. No one else is able to read your pages because that information is for your eyes only (we'll get into how biometrics can authenticate blockchain later in this chapter). It's incredibly difficult to steal the information out of your pages because the book is replicated across 7 billion people.

As Patientory doesn't put data on the blockchain, it's important to think of our utilization of blockchain technology as a decentralized storage system. Once the blockchain system is integrated with the hospital medical records, the data is encrypted and shared so that the Patientory network basically acts like road signs for queries. My goal is to provide patients instant access to their data.

The right place, at the right time

I would say that my early adoption of blockchain in the healthcare world was part luck and part fate. I believe I was in the proverbial "right place at the right time" and had the opportunity to put two disparate technologies together to try to help more people, which has always been my goal in life. I never thought that I would be growing an emerging industry as the Founder and CEO of a startup.

I saw the rise of digital healthcare startups in 2011, which led me to work in the field. At one point, I began to hear about Bitcoin in some of the cutting-edge industry press. They hadn't looked deeply into the connection to EMR (electronic medical records) field at the time; neither had I. But I did start digging into cryptography, and researched different types of technologies. A note about bitcoin here. *Bitcoin* refers to the system of bitcoin, which is a unit of currency you can use to pay for a haircut (we'll get into that in a minute). No one owns Bitcoin, the technology, which is now referred to as Blockchain.

Suddenly I had begun to look at two platforms to solve this problem of bringing together disparate systems using ledgers, which is essentially what blockchain is. I dove into the problem of the aggregation of digital medical records. And when I investigated this, I ended up coming across blockchain as a potential solution. Blockchain is essentially an electronic transaction method that keeps a record of transactions as they happen. Each file is given a unique identifier, a person. It's like checking out a book in a library; there's a record stored of everyone who has used it. This is an entire new world of how we're managing data.

The difference between blockchain and cryptocurrency

Basically, blockchain is the architecture that allows cryptocurrency to exist. Cryptocurrency and blockchain are meant to be inclusive technologies that are transforming the way we do business globally. By inclusive I mean they don't discriminate. They're blind to gender, race, social status, and your income. Cryptocurrency can give unbanked people the ability to have assets. A lot of people are unbanked for lots of different reasons, like refugees, for example. At the moment, other countries are more progressive in their implementation than America, but that can change at any time.

Patientory steps in to use blockchain and cryptocurrency to pair the user and their data so they can use the information to receive the best

possible healthcare. I think the biggest mystery I run into when I try to explain blockchain and cryptocurrency to people I interact with—whether VCs, investors or vendors—all boils down to one core idea:

Through blockchain, you're able to be the master of your own secured data.

As I mentioned earlier, a kind of cryptocurrency called bitcoin was invented by Stoshi Nakamoto. The unknown person or group invented the "peer-to-peer electronic cash system" and issued a white paper in 2008 in response to the crash that occurred in the financial markets at that time. In response, Nakamoto designed a blockchain database, a distributed database, containing a continuously-growing list of data records secured from revision and tampering, and capped at 21 million coins. Bitcoin turned ten in October of 2018. By that time, its mysterious architect had ,turned the concept and a 9-page white paper entitled "Bitcoin: A Peer-to-Peer Electronic Cash System" into a $200 billion economy with 2,000 kinds of cryptocurrencies currently worldwide, hosted on about 15,000 exchanges with a potential to transform the financial industry and other areas of our economy.

What makes cryptocurrency so secure?

"It's like signing for a package at your doorstep before passing it on to the next address with the entire delivery history recorded and encrypted securely. In this way, transactions can be verified without a central party, and owners are blocked from sending the same digital coin to more than one recipient."[3]

Cryptocurrency's blockchain, the shared data, is an accounting ledger

---

[3] https://www.scmp.com/tech/article/2170894/bitcoin-turns-10-how-everything-started-satoshi-nakamotos-9-page-white-paper

that keeps track of every transaction that the particular cryptocurrency has had. This data is also decentralized on a number of network computers called "nodes." When a transaction takes place, the nodes verify the transaction's validity (which means the person spending the cryptocurrency owns the cryptocurrency). A subset of nodes compete to package these transactions as valid and they're put into "blocks," which adds them into a chain of previous "blocks" or valid transactions. The owners of the nodes are called miners, and successfully adding blocks means that the miner earns more cryptocurrency. The first block in the initial blockchain was created by Nakamoto and is known as the Genesis Block in reference to bitcoin.

So, what makes blockchain special? It's a list or ledger of encrypted transactions, that once created, cannot be changed and is, therefore, trusted. When trust is codified in software there's no need to rely on third parties. This matters because it makes blockchain permanent and unchangeable. So when data is written, it's written only one time and read-only. Another benefit is that blockchain can be as long as it needs to be, having countless numbers of chronically linked blocks in the chain. Moreover, each completed block that enters the chain contains irreversible data.

Security lies in the fact that blockchain is stored on decentralized servers, so no central server holds the records. This fact allows trust between known and unknown parties who are accessing the data. So this means that trust is decentralized, meaning you won't have to go to "a bank" to get money anymore. Therefore, no central authority is needed to process and validate transactions, a service only performed by banks in the past. Instead, trust is electronically embedded in the software foundation.

Potential applications include the potential to transform significant areas of healthcare by increasing interoperability, the ability of computer systems or software to exchange and make use of information—bringing efficiency to processes, and employing smart contracts while still maintaining security and privacy. It can also offer technological solutions to the present gaps in health data interoperability.

With today's healthcare information infrastructure, patients don't own their current information. For instance, blockchain can promote interoperability through collaborative version control by ensuring that each participant in the network has a record of transactions occurring on the network. And it can potentially eliminate or reduce the costs and reliance on intermediaries. For example, the current legacy infrastructure systems known as EMRs (electronic medical records), Epic being one of the most prominent and successful in the past 30 years, created walled gardens, making it difficult to retrieve and access medical information.

Blockchain will also be a new foundation for pharmaceutical drug supply chain provenance and integrity. Now, companies will be able to track medication distribution at different stages of the supply chain, including at the drug level, to authenticate prescriptions, ensure a chain-of-custody log, and enhance transparency of components during the manufacture of medications. It will also allow consumers to track pharmaceutical products from the manufacturer throughout the supply chain to their home.

But that's not all. Blockchain will be able to provide innovative solutions for clinical trials and research by supporting safer, faster, trusted and more efficient clinical trials that will eradicate fraudulent modification of data. And it will help with professional credentialing because all records are stored on blockchain.

The result of these many benefits will be to eliminate the current inefficient system of identification, coverage proof, delivery documentation, and gaps that span from miscoding to inefficient appeal flow and poor interoperability.

Blockchain, my story

"A vehicle for trust; an infrastructure for value."

If I could use one word to describe blockchain, it would be transformational. I didn't start to formulate blockchain's application in healthcare until late 2015 and early 2016, after incorporating Patientory and taking it from idea to business. I had been formulating the business model and the mission statement and pretty much dreaming about what that company would look like almost a year before. I did a lot of research myself and also educated myself about how to best achieve a system that would keep healthcare data personal and able to be used to deliver premium healthcare all over the world. I knew the ultimate goal; I just hadn't found a way that we could actually integrate the foundational electronic system of our country where EMRs don't want to give up their data.

So I had a problem to solve when blockchain came about. At the time, though, I was still more focused on the business side of things. And my day-to-day was less about the architecture of the technical side of things and more about focusing on the nuts and bolts through application program interfaces (APIs).

When we were out fundraising and contemplating crowdfunding I realized that we really needed to figure out how to position the company to pay for our launch. That's when I really had to sit down and think about how blockchain would impact my company and how the feedback would be measured in the marketplace. It all started in late 2016 and early 2017, because Sean Wilkinson, who now sits on my board of advisors, said that a white paper with demonstration of the product would be all I needed to get people interested, create a community, and launch a crowdfunding sale. So I wrote the white paper. From the creation of that document and front-end I had been working on previously, I was able to market the idea and raise funds.

In the paper, I proposed a SaaS business model, which means we sell software to healthcare organizations where patients and consumers can download a free app. So our platform is based on what is called a "freemium" model. Essentially clients (like hospitals) and consumers of healthcare pay for services within the app. The analytic software we sell to healthcare service clients is built on the PTOYNetwork blockchain network, a healthcare specific blockchain open-source network, where we invite those healthcare companies to become members of our network to secure their data by running a node as well as use our software. The network is free to join.

In addition, I established a nonprofit arm that deals with a lot of the challenges of creating a product for an industry that doesn't exist at the moment. The goal of the Patientory Association is to help foster collaboration and adoption of emerging technology in healthcare. We really want to assist with emerging technology adoption in the healthcare space. So we have a team all over the world in different countries who serve in more of a business development capacity. It's a new concept for the world.

I believe that blockchain will play an increasingly significant role in healthcare IT and bring beneficial change and new efficiencies to every stakeholder in the ecosystem. It's vitally important that healthcare organizations understand the core of blockchain technology to ensure they're ready for the changes the technology entails.

The result will be a new generation of powerful, blockchain-based applications that will shape the next era of business in healthcare. For blockchain to fulfill its potential in healthcare, it must be based on standards to assure the compatibility and interoperability within the siloed healthcare system landscape.

Indeed the application of blockchain across societies will unlock many new business models similar to how the Internet created many new ways of people being able to transfer value and communicate with each other.

How do you pay for a haircut with crypto?

In May 2010, Laszlo Hanyecz, a Florida-based programmer, spent 10,000 bitcoins on two Papa John's pizzas, in the first known commercial transaction using bitcoin. At today's rate, those pizzas cost nearly 64 million dollars.[4]

The adoption of crypto has been slow. In 2017, when we had the big bitcoin surge, we had around 20,000 vendors in Atlanta accepting crypto for services, including local gas stations, pizza shops, and food trucks. One of the local barber shops here in Atlanta is owned by a Black male. He was one of the first to take on crypto in his barber shop and accept them as payment for haircuts.

How do you pay for a haircut with crypto? Usually the process involves a transfer using Coinbase. Another company in the space, called BitPay, started out here in Atlanta and was domiciled in an office in

---

[4] https://www.scmp.com/tech/article/2170894/bitcoin-turns-10-how-everything-started-satoshi-nakamotos-9-page-white-paper

our building at Atlanta Tech Village. BitPay, similar to PayPal, also has an integration for businesses so they can integrate Bitpay into their systems in order to accept crypto payments through them. There are many crypto third-party payment platforms today.

Basically you can pay with crypto using a cell phone or a computer. Crypto is a mobile digital transaction using ledger technology. So when you're at the barber shop and after your haircut, you can place your phone on a reader that accepts the crypto you've stored in your digital wallet, such as BitPay.

There are different types of digital wallets. There are cold storage wallets, currently the safest way to store cryptocurrency, where you essentially place your digital currency on a remote drive and store it in a secure facility.

Digital mobile wallets have websites where you can go online and sign up for, let's say a Coinbase account, which is a crypto currency exchange based in San Francisco. Over the past twelve months Coinbase has registered 8 million new users[5] and is currently the world's largest Bitcoin (BTC) broker.[6] Currently, Coinbase sells bitcoin, ethereum, litecoin, and bitcoin cash. Facebook is due to come out with their crypto currency called libra in the coming year.

Like other commodities in the U.S., users of crypto can buy and sell the currency on crypto exchanges. The exchanges and multiple third-party companies that have emerged in the past three to five years has made it easier for consumers to get ahold of crypto and be able to make transactions with them.

---

[5] https://cointelegraph.com/news/coinbase-added-8-million-new-users-in-the-past-year

[6] https://www.buybitcoinworldwide.com/exchanges/

Facebook is the first company out of the Big Four—Google, Apple, Facebook, and Amazon (GAFA)—to embrace cryptocurrency, which has, of course, flustered the government because with the notoriety and the power of Facebook, the soon-to-be-released libra will be competing with the U.S. dollar and other government-issued currency. So how will the U.S. government look at crypto from a regulatory standpoint and an economic standpoint? What will be the effects on cryptocurrency's value when it's owned and issued by a large corporation and its governors: a Swiss group of 28 members, including Facebook subsidiary Calibra, Uber, PayPal, Mastercard, Visa, Spotify, and other household names in tech and finance? What are the threats that this kind of currency can have over the long term?

As you can see, there really isn't a framework out there for this new technology at the moment. So it's been really difficult even for startups like Patientory to kick off our own currency because of these regulatory hurdles and just lack of knowledge about the topic by our own government leaders who need to create these policies.

Cryptocurrency in Healthcare

In 2019, there has been an increase in awareness of cryptocurrency in the healthcare field. Our company uses biometrics to really secure data to make theft and forgery a thing of the past because trust and security is everything. As a result, crypto is the safest currency around, in my opinion. Biometrics ensure that the people trying to hack into your cell phone can't get a "key" to give them access to your money or data. Within biometrics specifically, iris recognition is used to verify identity.

Cryptocurrency helps to revolutionize healthcare as a means to quantify and add value to transactions. This is the first time in history when a commodity and currency are one and the same. The PTOY token, when purchased by patients of healthcare providers on exchange platforms, will be able to rent health record and information storage and execute payments. For enterprises, it will also be used to initiate smart contracts and monitor storage as well as serve as an incentivization currency. Today, PTOY is found on exchange platforms. Different platforms are deemed better, based upon their trade volume. Trade volume is the total number of shares or contracts that were traded during a given period for a specified security.

Binance is one of the world's biggest crypto-to-crypto exchanges, which takes pride in low transaction fees. Binance was started in 2017 by Changpeng Zhao and Yi He who started their careers in crypto through OKCoin exchange. Binance, known for being the fastest and most liquid of all the exchange platforms, was intended to serve as China's primary bitcoin exchange platform. However, over time, they've expanded beyond China.

Coinbase, on the other hand, is a broker exchange platform founded in San Francisco, California by Brian Armstrong and Fred Ehrsam. A broker exchange buys a cryptocurrency for a customer rather than bringing buyers and sellers together like most other exchanges do. In 2017, Coinbase was the first exchange company to be valued at over one billion USD.

Both platforms have been extremely successful and are relatively new exchange platforms. Even though both platforms are large, Binance is the larger exchange platform out of the two exchanges. Binance and Coinbase differ in the type of currency services they provide. Coinbase offers fiat trading services which allows users to buy and sell cryptocurrency with fiat currency. Fiat currency is the name given to any money declared by a government to be legal tender—for example, the U.S. Dollar, the Mexican Peso, or the Japanese Yen. Many beginners find that this method of trading is easier for them to start with because they can find everything they need on the platform without having to visit other exchanges before they start trading. In comparison, Binance doesn't offer fiat trading; however, they do offer a wider range of cryptocurrencies because they're strictly involved in cryptocurrency trading. For more advanced traders, Binance is a great option because their coin selection is the best on the market. Lastly, cryptocurrency exchanges charge different fees. Coinbase charges a fee of 1.49% that can increase up to 3.99% if the trade is made with a credit card. On the other hand, Binance doesn't charge a fee for deposits and withdrawals and only charges a fee of .01% for trades.

Why is crypto 'disrupting'?

Because Facebook is issuing cryptocurrency, one particular argument our government touts is the idea that Facebook wants to become a bank and if that's what they want to become, then they need to be regulated like a bank. But they're missing the point. The banking business model and the cryptocurrency business model have nothing in common. As I mentioned earlier in the book, crypto was created as a kind of rebellion against the status quo.

It's not a surprise that they would jump to this conclusion. Facebook, with their libra token, are going to have custody of the assets of their billion-plus users. Facebook's maintains that they aren't really a bank, but more of a third-party vendor of crypto. However, the argument the government poses is that Facebook's proposal is actually the potential classification of a bank.

They then likened Facebook's initiatives with crypto to scrip, which is a kind of currency that has been around for hundreds of years and can only be exchanged in company stores owned by employers. But crypto isn't company scrip. This is a valid argument wrought on government's control of checks and balances to influence a corporate entity regarding currency. And this poses the question, how does a government serve the people on a financial level if the people begin to take their finances out of the hands of government regulation? Here's a cautionary tale on what crypto definitely isn't.

"Ocasio-Cortez references previous instances of people being paid in corporate-controlled currency, known as 'scrip' -- a very dark history there. Company scrip is a company-controlled currency. Back in the day, if you worked for Acme Co., you lived in Acme housing and shopped at the Acme store with Acme-issued 'dollars.' In 'company towns' where one firm employed most of the working population, there would be only company stores.

Often, workers had to buy work tools, groceries, and everything else with scrip at the company store, and often at higher prices than they could afford, leading to a cycle of debt.

It's now illegal to pay workers this way. In 1955, Tennessee Ernie Ford had a hit with the song 'Sixteen Tons,' whose coal-mining narrator lamented: 'Saint Peter don't call me 'cause I can't go/I owe my soul to the company store.'"[7]

Another aspect of crypto is how it would be valued on the international stage. Crypto is crypto until you convert it to fiat. At that point, the crypto value will be determined for each government-issued currency.

Europe is the most advanced right now with their incorporation of

---

[7] https://www.bnnbloomberg.ca/ocasio-cortez-compares-facebook-s-libra-to-company-issued-scrip-1.1288618

cryptocurrency in their financial system. They actually have bitcoin ATMs where you can buy and sell bitcoin. But the end result is the same as the U.S. Using cryptocurrency is going to be dependent on whether or not the merchant you frequent has adopted the type of crypto you own.

To make transactions with cryptocurrency you need a wallet. As I touched on earlier, a cryptocurrency wallet is the software that holds the secret keys you use to digitally sign your cryptocurrency transactions' distributed ledgers. Those keys are the only way to validate your ownership of the digital assets, and their possession allows you to execute transactions to transfer those assets or change them. Keys are specific to specific currencies bitcoin for bitcoin, ethereum for ethereum. Keys are the glue that holds the crypto ecosystem together.

Crypto wallets are essentially markers of the digital address of the blockchain where the particular crypto resides. These wallets hold the keys to your financial transactions—spending, buying, and selling them. Lose the keys and you lose control over your digital money or other digital assets. There are two kinds of crypto wallets—hardware and software (also known as cold and hot storage, respectively). Coinbase provides hot storage wallets which can then be broken into online wallets and client-side wallets managed by them on their computer or smartphone. Cold storage wallets can be purchased with the software already installed on them; these kinds of devices are sold by vendors such as Trezor and Ledger.

Facebook currency is a permissioned currency, meaning that it's controlled by the over 100 companies that Facebook has brought together to create their cryptocurrency. Together, Facebook has over a hundred million dollars in assets. To be a part of their consortium or association, the players have to pay $10 million. Because no one controls bitcoin, it's a permissionless currency, so no one controls bitcoin. It's traded on crypto exchanges, and countries around the world are currently adding them to their markets.

As I mentioned earlier, governments are having a hard time understanding and responding to their regulation. Representative Barbara Waters (D) California opened up a recent House Financial Services Committee meeting that examined Facebook's proposed cryptocurrency and its impact on consumers and investors and the American financial system. Before Calibra CEO David Marcus testified about Facebook's proposed digital currency libra, she had these words: "Facebook is intent on creating a new global financial system that is due to rival the U.S. dollar. They have failed to keep customers' information private on a scale similar to Equifax." She went on to suggest sponsoring a "Keep Big Tech Out of Finance Act."

It's important that regulators embrace the technology and be onboard with it for us to really see mass adoption of cryptocurrency. In order to keep up with the rest of the world and have crypto ATMs available at your local grocery store, we need initial infrastructure for the transfer of value using these digital commodities. But, it seems that its implementation is currently facing a strong headwind.

I believe the disruption that everyone is feeling is really a shift that's happening in society around how we look at business and the concepts of globalization and making the world smaller through network effects.

Get in the game

So, how can you as a minority female entrepreneur become a part of this movement?

There are many ways to stay connected with what's going on in cryptocurrency and blockchain. I use a variety of networking groups to stay up-to-date on all the developments in the field. I've included a list of some of these resources at the back of the book for your easy reference. I've also found it important to be part of a group of people who are seeking answers in business and blockchain.

I also recommend looking for local groups and meetups in your area. They've been a great source of knowledge for me, and I highly recommend finding one in order to stay connected to the developments in the technology and network with like-minded people. In Atlanta, the Atlanta Blockchain Meetup has over 3,000 members. They meet in the Atlanta Tech Village space where they now hold their meetings once a month to talk about case studies, give updates about the industry, and help the general public understand the technology and its advancements.

Blockchain & cryptocurrency myths

Cryptocurrency "is not money"

Money is used to avoid the inconvenience of barter systems. In that regard, cryptocurrency is definitely a form of money. In fact, cryptocurrency is the most advanced form of asset in human history that can represent both a commodity and currency. It's a true transformation of how human beings have been transferring value for over 3,000 years.

"Over the course of history, different forms of money have appeared and disappeared from the market, based on their economic properties. Because all economic value is subjective to the individual, as the great Austrian Economist Carl Menger explained to the world in his seminal work *Principles of Economics*, a money's value is contingent on the trust of its users to maintain purchasing power and salability across time.

"'Bitcoin is the hardest money ever invented,' according to Austrian economist Saifedean Ammous, because 'growth in its value cannot possibly increase its supply; it can only make the network more secure and immune to attack.'....The ability to inflate—and thus destroy—the value of the dollar rests solely with the Federal Reserve's printing presses."[8]

Cryptocurrency is "highly volatile"

"Bitcoin's volatility derives from the fact that its supply is utterly inflexible and not responsive to demand changes."[9]
—Saifedean Ammous

Bitcoin is still *"the best performing asset over the last ten years."*[10]
—Anthony Pompliano

"Blockchain & cryptocurrency can facilitate unlawful behavior and illegal activity"

Actually, in my experience, blockchain and cryptocurrency have really given people a voice and made transactions totally transparent in a way that the cash system doesn't. People like to say that crypto and blockchain and bitcoin are used by the black market, the underworld and drug traffickers. But no one talks about how the U.S. dollar is the number one source for drug trafficking.[11]

Bitcoin is tied to a ledger identification which is traceable, and hardly

---

[8] https://fee.org/articles/trump-is-all-wrong-about-Bitcoin/

[9] https://twitter.com/saifedean

[10] https://www.cnbc.com/video/2018/11/26/bitcoin-will-end-down-at-85-percent-of-previous-highs-says-expert.html

[11] https://ips-dc.org/drug_trafficking_and_money_laundering/

the place criminals would want to conduct illegal transactions.

"Blockchain isn't safe"

With a move toward ease of access to data and decentralization in a world where security continues to pose a serious risk, blockchain is becoming the answer to many industry-wide obstacles.

"Healthcare systems are being targeted by cyberattacks because their legacy infrastructures make data vulnerable. In 2017, the ransomware "WannaCry" crippled the National Health Service (NHS) in the United Kingdom and affected over 150 countries. In 2018 and 2019 respectively, hackers broke into Singapore's government health database,[12] and, most recently, the HIV status of over 14,000 people leaked online,"[13] Singapore authorities say.

Given that blockchain is a distributed ledger technology and doesn't require third-party interventions, it allows institutions to decentralize their databases. By using blockchain, healthcare systems can significantly reduce their risk of being subjected to cyberthreats simply because it would take too much time and energy for hackers to access all of the nodes within the network and infect the system.

It's highly important to create an environment where clinicians, administrators, and patients (also known as consumers of healthcare) know that their privacy and data are protected. Such an ecosystem can be enabled by blockchain, either by allowing users to own their information by joining the chain or by helping hospitals to secure their servers and distribute the data on a network.

---

[12] https://www.bbc.com/news/world-asia-44900507

[13] https://www.cnn.com/2019/01/28/health/hiv-status-data-leak-singapore-intl/index.html

Future of blockchain & cryptocurrency

Welcome to the new trust economy

Blockchain has been adopted by governments all over the world. For example, Estonia runs a distributed ledger technology to secure their citizens' data and healthcare medical information. We also see countries and cities like Dubai, which has put out initiatives to make certain that they're the first city to run solely on blockchain by 2021. Blockchain is the Web 3.0, as many would say. I see the future of blockchain as another layer that adds to the foundation of the Internet we recognize today. Blockchain will certainly be commonplace in how we're going to be doing business and how we will make transactions in the near future.

In healthcare, I see blockchain as a solution to the increase in transactional costs and as an aid to the clinical side in terms of cost savings for patients. We're also seeing an increase in chronic illnesses, especially in the U.S. Right now, over two-thirds of the U.S. population currently has one or more chronic illness, which again is contributing to a rise in costs for healthcare. So the goal for many entrepreneurs in the space, like myself, who are focused on digital health technology, is really about providing solutions where our healthcare system can run efficiently with much healthier populations. I believe blockchain is the technology that will make these goals possible. For example, Patientory is a fully HIPAA-compliant, cybersecurity healthcare data solution that allows users to securely store, transfer, and receive actionable insights into their health information on PTOYNetwork blockchain network.

Our healthcare is broken. A lot of people really agree with that statement—from clinicians to people on the technology side. We're still running on siloed technology. Our doctors are still faxing, so healthcare hasn't been a front runner in the early adoption of technology. They're not mavericks in the field as other industries have demonstrated. We definitely have to get to a point where we have a technology-enabled healthcare system that's more efficient for everyone. However, the workforce is definitely what works in healthcare today. We may have some nursing shortages in rural areas, but we do have great accredited providers for the population as it stands today.

At Patientory, we have two entities. One is a nonprofit that's focused on helping healthcare companies and hospitals adopt emerging technologies (you can find more about that at patientory.com); we have over 11 ambassadors worldwide that consult with healthcare organizations on best practices. We also host an annual summit where we deep dive into how blockchain can transform the healthcare industry. Patientory, Inc. is our for-profit entity that provides consulting and software for healthcare organizations.

A curated healthcare experience

> *"Blockchain has the power to reduce costs and increase operational efficiency; build trust while improving the quality of comprehensive care, and empower individuals to take charge of their health. It's time for us to reimagine the future of healthcare information technology."*[14]
>
> — Blockchain: Unlocking Healthcare Data to
> Empower Patients and Improve Care

---

[14] https://www.himss.org/news/blockchain-unlocking-healthcare-data-empower-patients-and-improve-care

It's time for us to reimagine the future of healthcare information technology. More specifically, it's time for us to rethink the management of personal health information (i.e., data from electronic health records [EHRs] and wearable devices). Data will continue to drive the technology that's becoming increasingly intertwined in our everyday lives, and this remains especially true for healthcare.

From Internet-enabled medical devices to fitness trackers, developments in digital health are creating new opportunities for comprehensive patient care and raising new questions about the ethical management of healthcare data. At Patientory, we believe the correct application of blockchain technology will allow us to effectively take advantage of these opportunities and provide answers to some of these questions.

Our biggest challenge in healthcare is the lack of infrastructure, communication between the different healthcare computer systems, and just the monopoly that certain healthcare technology vendors have, almost like they own your healthcare information.

To address this, we're basically creating a highway, as we like to call it, by using blockchain to make the data that exists now available not only to the patients because it's their data but also to interested stakeholders, such as researchers, care providers, and secondary care providers, including specialists and emergency rooms, that would benefit from having that data immediately accessible.

In an ideal world, we would have a connected healthcare network and ecosystem. The Patientory app integrates with this network to make your data available to you so that wherever you go, you'll have access to that historical information. We're also using analytics to help the individual receive better personalized care to feel empowered and make more informed healthcare decisions. The core of our for-profit really focuses on the administration, the tracking, and the integration of data, and how we're going to create the next phase of data integration from the legacy siloed systems that exist today in the healthcare space.

The need for this kind of integration is huge because of all the examples people share about the outrageous ways they've had to be their own healthcare advocate. For example, I heard of a lady who needed minor surgery. However, her primary care doctor didn't speak to the specialist yet and there she sat at the hospital. Not everyone was on the same page, so she didn't have all the answers she needed before having the surgery. She Googled for answers to her healthcare questions because no one else could answer them. This was information she needed yesterday. **Googling for your own healthcare answers while you're in the hospital is unacceptable.**

On the flip side, blockchain has the capability to help people in need get the answers and resources they require immediately. A great example of this is how blockchain has been used globally as a tracking device where refugees have registered. These unbankable citizens are from countries in the midst of turmoil and have fled, causing them to lose all forms of identification. Governments in Europe have been able to track these people using iris recognition technology which we use on our platform for identity management. Refugees receive financial aid within these refugee camps powered by this iris recognition technology.

The idea I would be able to go somewhere to gain access to money through an iris-scan, makes the idea of not carrying around a purse even more worthwhile. Little did I know that I'd be incorporating the technology at Patientory. In late 2018, when we started to speak with IrisGuard, we were in the UK showcasing, and one of their co-founders came up to me and mentioned that he was interested in healthcare.

They have been around for over ten years. He mentioned that they'd worked with the UN and the World Food Program to provide iris recognition.

For these kinds of humanitarian programs, they use iris technology as a tracking device to register refugees and unbankable citizens. IrisGuard has been able to track everything from identity to financial transactions using their technology. They mentioned that they were looking to expand into healthcare and approached us, saying that they thought blockchain was the next evolution for their technology.

They were excited about the PTOYNetwork blockchain network and its capabilities. So we partnered with them. We brought their iris technology to our blockchain which will enable more privacy and private key pair functions, data management for our users and for our enterprise customers. Our goal is to test pilot a study with over 200 patients to begin to understand how to implement our technology into this very large network.

In the best applications of blockchain, you don't even know it's there. Some developers call it the "truffle theory." The best development of blockchain I've found is like a truffle with a little bit of flavor. You don't really need to be too heavy handed with blockchain. When you download the Patientory App, you'll see it has components of a cryptocurrency wallet, but we try to really create a seamless experience where users don't feel like they're using a blockchain platform. It's more like using WhatsApp or any other app that's out there in the App Store. It's something really specific to the user's healthcare where they can actually aggregate a lot of the other healthcare apps they use—like their devices, and their Fitbit to better curate a healthcare experience.

We're empowering users to have all their healthcare data in one place.

That way, they can easily reference and share information with their providers and anyone else they wish. In addition, we're looking into patient updates, kind of like what Google Health and the Microsoft Health Vault tried to do in a Personal Health Record (PHR) about five years ago. We create an interface where the user will be able to upload and organize their data and then format it in a way that would still be useful. That way they'll have the empowered experience of knowing and having all the healthcare data they need to make informed healthcare decisions.

Despite incredible advancements over the last decade in converting paper healthcare records into digital data, the vast majority of consumers lack access to their electronic medical records. Sadly, many people cannot manage their healthcare records any better than they could a decade ago or even three decades ago. While it can be easy for some to point the finger at the bureaucracy and red tape of healthcare institutions, the truth is that many of these institutions would like to share data with their patients but don't have a secure and easy way to do this.

This challenging dynamic exists because many medical providers use different electronic health record (EHR) systems that actually may not be able to communicate with one another easily. The resulting situation has become a significant problem where patients are caught in the middle of the healthcare industry's lack of interoperability and without solutions that can provide patients accessible and secure healthcare data.

Challenges for comprehensive care

Despite the advent of EHRs, medical records still suffer from a lack of interoperability. IT systems are often siloed and unique to the provider, which means a large amount of time and resources are spent simply requesting, sending, and compiling health information. This makes it challenging to create a comprehensive picture of an individual's health across multiple providers, especially when there are variations in insurance coverage and geographic location over time.

Additionally, we are starting to see an increase in clinicians relying on patient-generated health data in conjunction with clinical data.[15] This type of information includes health histories, symptoms, lifestyle choices, biometrics, etc., and can better inform care decisions because the data provides valuable insight into an individual's overall health and well-being in between medical visits. While patient portals and EHRs allow for a small portion of this data to be compiled, today's technologies could be leveraged more effectively to improve health outcomes.

Challenges for Healthcare Data Management

In addition to being siloed, legacy healthcare IT systems are often aging and lacking in robust cybersecurity measures. Hospitals are particularly appealing targets for cyberattacks[16] because their daily operations rely heavily on up-to-date information from electronic medical records, and stolen health information is worth ten times more than a credit card number on the black market[17]. The more an EHR is fragmented across multiple providers, the higher the patient's risk of personal data being

---

[15] https://patientory.com/blog/2018/12/20/the-true-potential-of-patient-generated-health-data/

[16] https://patientory.com/blog/2018/11/01/blockchain-the-defender-of-healthcare-organizations-against-cybercriminals/

[17] https://www.reuters.com/article/us-cybersecurity-hospitals-idUSKCN0HJ21I20140924

exposed to people with malicious intent.

Since all of a provider's EHRs are stored in one place, a successful breach will give a hacker access to all of that information at once. What's especially troubling about this is that individuals have little control over the storage of their own personal health data and can do little to prevent this. There's an overall lack of patient control when it comes to the access and use of their own medical data, and this reflects broader societal questions about data management. Legislation, including HIPAA, simply hasn't caught up to the growing role of data in our lives.

Blockchain as a solution

When applied to EHRs, blockchain can potentially address these issues. A blockchain consists of encrypted blocks of data that are immutable and linked together chronologically in a chain. In a healthcare setting, these blocks of data could be doctor's appointments, surgical procedures, x-ray images, prescriptions, blood test results, patient-generated health data, etc. Copies of the blockchain would be distributed across a specified network of users, and any additions to the chain would be updated for all users in real time. Individuals would be in charge of sharing the decryption key for their own associated blocks of data with their chosen healthcare provider(s).

With a distributed application like Patientory's, individuals would have access to a comprehensive picture of their health that includes compiled data from EHRs and wearable devices. [18] Breaking the silos of traditional medical record storage would not only make the process of sharing EHRs significantly easier, but also result in more robust

----

[18] https://patientory.com/features/

security. By integrating with PTOYNetwork distributed and decentralized blockchain network, our application is able to adhere to both HIPAA and robust security standards.

That's why Patientory developed a distributed application DApp solution that provides individual consumers with quick, easy, and secure access to their healthcare data. As the industry leader for DApp blockchain solutions, Patientory recently developed the first version of its beta DApp for consumers.

Patientory's DApp leverages blockchain technology. The open and secure technology captures transaction records on blocks that are connected and stores them on a distributed and encoded database that acts as a ledger. Blockchain has incredible security benefits as the records are spread across a replicated database network in which all the databases are in sync. Users, however, can only access the blocks to which they have permission. All the transactions that happen over blockchain are date and time stamped.

As for DApps, they're applications that interface with blockchains that aren't stored or controlled by a single entity or in a single location. This means that a particular EHR or healthcare provider doesn't solely control an individual's healthcare data, thus allowing for more efficient, user-friendly, and secure sharing of healthcare data among different providers and EHR platforms.

This new DApp solution was created from research data Patientory has collected over the past few years regarding the challenges that healthcare consumers face regularly and how these challenges have evolved over time. With the DApp solution, Patientory's goal is to create a one-stop-shop solution for healthcare consumers where they can access their health information, engage in health-related transactions, and become empowered to improve their health by having the necessary data and tools to do so.

From Patientory's beta testing of its new beta app and the subsequent user survey, it's evident that the DApp is meeting a clear and immediate need for the consumer market. Despite only being a beta product, the vast majority of users found the DApp to not only serve as a valuable healthcare solution but also function as an excellent tool for managing fitness and diet. Along with the value of the app, most individuals found the user experience to be very engaging and relevant, which is an indicator for repeated and ongoing use. Lastly, the back-end software of the app performed well, according to most users, with the speed of the app and ease and time of install getting high marks.

I see the future of blockchain in healthcare at Patientory, where we empower users with actionable insight and ownership of their own health data to meet health goals, make more informed healthcare decisions, and live healthier, longer lives.

A bullish case for cryptocurrency

There are a few reasons bitcoin could go to $100,000. When we went through the financial crises in 2000 and 2008, the Federal Reserve printed money. They called it quantitative easing, but it's just an experiment. They didn't have any history with it, but they were desperate to hold up the economy. So they decided to print money. When the mortgage crisis hit, people believed that the real estate market would always go up. They cited history saying the real estate market had never crashed. And of course the experts, the scientists, were wrong.

But I believe at some point, the printing of fiat money backed by nothing in order to pay off your own debts with your own money is essentially like using a monopoly board with unlimited money. It's not pretty when that system fails—like it has in Venezuela or Zimbabwe––or suffers the kind of inflation that Argentina or Turkey have experienced.

Money used to be backed by gold. If people start to question the debt the U.S. has taken on, there would be a huge run for gold. But potentially people would begin looking at other monetary systems that aren't controlled by a central government to hedge the risk involved in relying on the volatility of government-backed securities.

I think the bullish case for bitcoin is, in part, based on the people's confidence in the financial system, in fiat money. There aren't many alternatives to fiat money, but only because there's a limited number of bitcoin. Because of that limited availability, bitcoin is the best option of the currency. There's not a lot of competition in terms of fiat money that governments print. If people's confidence transfers over from fiat money to bitcoin, we would see a big jump in value, just as we did when it ran up to $20,000.

> *"Blockchain is so profound it will do for trusted transactions what the internet did for information."*
>
> —Ginni Rometty, American business executive;
> current Chair, President, and CEO of IBM,
> and the first woman to head the company.

MINORITY & MINDSET

"Everyone can contribute to your success, even if they just show you what not to do."

—Chrissa McFarlane

My parents are immigrants from the Caribbean island of Jamaica. I was actually born in Jamaica but raised in New York City. As a little girl, I always dreamed about helping people and decided to go into medicine and become a surgeon. I went to a specialized science and technology high school because I was really strong in math and science growing up, so that career just made sense. As a result, I did research at a young age and seemed clinically inclined.

But, I never became a doctor. Instead, I became the Founder and CEO of Patientory, empowering end users globally with a secure platform to manage and transfer their health data to achieve actionable insights for improved health outcomes and well-being.

My journey illustrates a lot of the challenges that minority women go through to excel in their field. It also points out where I believe the dreams and hopes of the future lie for minority women and the Fourth Industrial Revolution. The formation of our future involves looking at the changing roles of women in society as well as the current and past climate for minority women in business.

I believe that we need more than simply sowing the entrepreneurial dream in our young women so that they feel empowered. We need to give them a roadmap to achieve the kind of confidence that leads to empowerment. To make that happen, it's important to reinforce a woman's self-worth so that no business situation leads them down the path to marginalization or disenfranchisement simply because those experiences feel uncomfortable and even unfamiliar. We sabotage ourselves when we let abusive people or situations take over our lives and worse yet, define our self-worth.

The early years

My experience in nurturing my self-awareness to build confidence began in 5th grade when my teacher, Mrs. White, gave me an early insight into how I would define myself. I believe it's important to receive these positive reinforcements about self-worth not only inside but also outside of the home. My teacher saw my potential and even likened me to Condoleezza Rice. Her attention to my abilities made me realize the importance of not only believing in my own intelligence and being comfortable with it but also believing in education as a way to a certain kind of freedom.

The most important part of minority and mindset is to never let a person who marginalizes you define you. When others notice and encourage our abilities, talents, and gifts (especially ones that we may be unaware of or even take for granted), insight and transformation happens. Because Mrs. White gave me the ability to self-educate and self-teach, my confidence increased because I didn't need others to help me discover my true self or guide me to my true calling. That's giving the wrong people too much power.

Beyond confidence and a good sense of self-worth, there's a combination of forces at play for Future Women. One key strength I noticed in my experience is that my education provided me the ability to take advantage of the changes that had occurred in society, allowing me to go for success in business in a way that my grandmother and mother never could. Before, women may have received a bachelor's degree or a master's degree and been a valued employee. But I'm striving and pushing through that barrier as Founder and CEO of my own company. There are many internal and external forces at work that allow me to push further to accomplish greater things than were possible before. One of the external forces that allowed me to push a little further was learning how to adapt when I moved from one country to another and, consequently, one school to another.

I began my education in Jamaica in a primary school. The images of my sobbing, teary-eyed classmates saying goodbye to me in Jamaica are ingrained in my memory to this day. I accompanied my mother and father to their home in the Bronx, filled with familiar copies of Angus Maciver books from my mother's time as a teacher in Jamaica, which predominantly followed the UK's system of education. Not only did I have to adjust to a new country, I also needed to adapt to a new way of being educated in the United States curriculum once I started school. Not to mention having to get used to a new, very cold climate!

Before I met Mrs. White when I was around eleven, I was a good student but more of an average performer, receiving Cs and B-minuses. During the year I was in Mrs. White's class, my behavior changed partly because of her encouragement that made me realize I could do better. So I believed her and wanted to do so. Not only that but she also made me see that I have the ability to thrive in that way. She just loved to celebrate her students and encourage them right where they were. Besides report cards, she gave out small tokens (maybe that's where my love of tokens started) and awards.

It seemed like I always came home holding some sort of certificate saying "outstanding" in reading or math. And each one of my certificates went in a special binder at home. My parents would always showcase them at their dinner parties with their friends. Mrs. White showed me my value in transformational ways that eventually fueled my growth.

Future women of today

FUTURE WOMAN MINDSET: Show value in transformational ways people have never seen before. (Arlan Hamilton, Founder Backstage Capital)

> *I have to keep doing this until we're no longer underestimated or underrepresented. That's the clear end goal.*
> —Arlan Hamilton, founder of Backstage Capital

I believe Arlan Hamilton is a great example of a minority woman who has demonstrated this mindset beautifully. She continually shows people their value in transformational ways they have never seen before. **Before Arlan founded Backstage Capital, she'd suffered homelessness and even ended up couch surfing while pitching her company idea— one that would meet the needs of minority entrepreneurs who were usually overlooked by venture capitalists.**

I had the opportunity of speaking with Arlan myself when pitching my company. Her take-charge attitude isn't compatible with someone who would ever be satisfied with the leftovers that traditional VCs seemed to only throw to minorities. She got tired of the same old story where female startup founders, people of color, and those in the LGBTQ community had to survive on the leftovers of traditional financing. She responded by founding Backstage Capital in 2015 to finance marginalized, minority seed-stage startups. Since then, the fund has about 30 employees and has invested roughly $5 million in over 100 startups headed by overlooked founders. Her passion for helping to transform the companies in which she invests is fueled partially because she's Black and also in the LGBTQ community.

In other words, it's personal. So how did this Future Woman find her inspiration to create Backstage Capital and lay herself on the line for the disenfranchised? And how did she gain the confidence necessary to build this kind of financial powerhouse?

As it turns out, Arlan noticed how celebrities began to invest in startups about a decade ago. Since she wanted to start her own company, this trend interested her enough to find out more about the people who invest in startups. What she uncovered blew her away. Not only were brown and Black founders underrepresented, they were actually undervalued as well. This discovery brought on the desire to do something big about reversing the trend and literally transforming the face, or I should say faces, of the startup world. Her raw confidence gave her a kind of peace with boldly challenging the status quo while championing diversity by filling the gaps in the funding of minority startups.

"There are definitely people who paved the way for what I do. But I think some of them were a little afraid to rock the boat, because it had been so difficult for them to get in. I was already dancing on the boat as I walked in," Hamilton said.

While pitching her idea to VCs, she didn't have any of the trappings of mainstream founders like a home, a trust-fund, or a college degree––forget Stanford.

"I was going toe-to-toe with people who had an unlimited amount of money, who could wine and dine their limited partners with lavish events and big productions," Hamilton said. "I would go home and my home would be the airport or a hotel or someone's couch, or an Airbnb that I scraped together the money for. And that's just not the story here with people starting funds," Hamilton said. "I don't recommend that you do that. But I feel like I was carving my way into a separate category, so I had to do it. There was no other way to break ground."[19]

Arlan basically advocates what my teacher Mrs. White helped me to understand—my self-confidence all boiled down to what I believed about myself. As a teacher, Mrs. White gave me another lesson in mindset: competence. If you don't know it, learn it.

FUTURE WOMAN MINDSET: If you don't know it, learn it.

At my old school, in previous grades, other girls got A's and B's. I remember back at that school, I always second-guessed myself and wondered if I didn't belong or that I was doing something wrong. I did my homework every night like all the other kids. But this wasn't really a new way for me to think about myself. This wasn't the first time I felt this way on my journey of acculturation.

My mindset defaulted to this kind of thinking during this period of adjustment to a new culture, an experience many immigrant children face at a young age. As a little girl in elementary school, I felt very different. Even though we lived in the "Jamaican section of the city," when I went to school, it was a melting pot of all cultures in the NYC borough, and I was often teased because of my accent. At one point, I felt as if I didn't belong, which made me overly shy, soft-spoken, and

---

[19] *Arlan Hamilton was homeless when she founded Backstage Capital for overlooked entrepreneurs.* latimes.com
https://www.latimes.com/business/la-fi-himi-arlan-hamilton-backstage-capital-20190512-story.html May, 2019. Accessed July 2019.

reserved, but that almost always equated to people as "good behavior."

Mrs. White made me feel like I'd come home to myself. She was also Jamaican and had gotten her master's in teaching. I remember her being very well-read and eloquent, definitely warm, and one of the more mature teachers in the school at the time. In fact, she reminded me of my mother, a woman of principle and very disciplined.

After improving my performance in Mrs. White's class, she later selected me for the gifted program. It was a way for high-achieving, inner-city students to receive the opportunity to transfer to an elite private school. Because she was encouraging, I always participated in the summer reading club, which my mother also required us to do every summer. The rewards definitely instilled a sense of purpose for accomplished work. So, the ability to be incentivized in school where there were prizes, pizza, and fun games helped in building the confidence I needed to thrive in school.

FUTURE WOMAN MINDSET: Nurture and protect your mindset like a little baby. Give it good care and feeding. (Farah Allen, Founder & CEO The Labz)

> *"I started The Labz for a couple of reasons. One was the lack of executive opportunities in the technology sector for me, as a Black woman."*[20]
>
> —Farah Allen, CEO of The Labz, an online platform making it easier for the creative community to determine ownership and percentage splits for future revenue.

---

[20] https://moguldom.com/203308/ip-protection-ceo-farah-allen-blockchain-the-labz-mogulwatch/

Farrah founded The Labz as an online platform where account holders can collaborate through the security of blockchain which, in turn, clarifies ownership and royalty percentage splits. The Labz website describes it best, "The Labz platform makes owning the rights to your work as easy as file sharing and writing lyrics."

Allen began her career as an IT consultant and security specialist and sought out guidance from accelerator programs like Digital Undivided and Comcast Universal The Farm. Not only did she gain traction by attending an accelerator program, she also grew her original $50,000 investment into a million-dollar company. Her software-as-a-service concept helped her take her place at the forefront of intellectual property (IP) protection.

> *"Protecting songwriters has been a problem since music started. I began my research into this issue about five years ago. We started developing the idea, doing our research, talking to the overall industry on a higher level, and then the laws started to change. Pushing the principles behind the Music Modernization Act started becoming popular and something organizations were trying to push through for regulation by the government. It made this issue more public and that was good for me and for The Labz because we were already solving a problem for which everyone was all of a sudden trying to find a solution. **Suddenly the industry was talking about something I had already figured out years ago — that creation, protection, and data should be collected at the very beginning of the song creation process.** I see creators as wanting to be creators and not the standard businesspeople. I created a technology where they are allowed to do that and the technology does the business part for them like any other industry."[21]*
>
> —Farrah Allen

---

[21] Ibid.

Farrah is an expert at putting the pieces together. Mrs. White would inspire this in me years later when she spoke at my Sweet Sixteen party, a Jamaican Quinceanera of sorts.

The Hollywood-themed party, complete with a red carpet and an entourage of eight girls and eight boys—which we called my court—took place at my church's event center and looked like a night at the Oscars. We even had a smoke machine. I wore a white Cinderella-dress with a tiara, of course, and changed into a peach dress later on in the night. The entertainment that evening included a DJ and balloons and even special Jamaican food catered by Patois, my mom and dad's restaurant.

After my court and I made our entrance on the red carpet, we wound our way through the event center to loud music before taking our seats on stage. I sat in the front and my court sat in a semi-circle behind me. An MC started off the night with introductions of everyone and then we prayed. Afterward, he called up my friend's dance troupe and they gave an off-the-hook performance in front of about fifty guests who sat at circular tables. My mother and women from our church community served the sit-down dinner. Dressed in black and white with little aprons, they darted about the tables seeing to it that everyone had their heart's desire. After dinner, the MC invited everyone to the dancefloor. Of course, we danced all night, laughed a lot, and there were a few speeches.

Mrs. White took the podium in her beautiful dress, it was as if the entire room went silent. She was a tall slender lady and her demeanor exuded confidence and respect. Her dress was always cultural; a floral dress resembling one an African royal high priestess would wear. Like I remembered years before in the classroom, she always brought an air of confidence that demanded the utmost attention. When she got the microphone situated, she took a beat and looked at the crowd over her reading glasses, nodding to a few people she knew from the community.

"I'm so proud of you today, Chrissa," she said, glancing over at me. "I remember the first day you walked into my class with your sharpened pencils, one of my only students to adhere to the dress code and wear the school's uniform. Most teachers have an eye for students that are different. But not every student changes the life of her teacher. That's rare and so are you. I had no idea how you'd go on to change my life too. Truly, there are no words to express what it is like to stand here today, seeing you as a young woman knowing what I know about your potential. I see you growing up to help others, Chrissa. That, I believe has been and will always be your calling. You have been such a role model for how to give back to society even at your young age."

I was amazed at how her words awakened something in my heart that wasn't there before. She saw me in a way I hadn't seen myself. She saw me as someone who could make a difference in this world. And because she'd said all that publicly, in front of everyone whom I loved and cared about, I guess I finally believed the good stuff about myself. She hadn't just spoken warm words of affection; her words had the air of a call to action.

Even today, I continue to strive way past mediocrity because of her belief in me. And I guess in that way, it's not surprising that I've become my own competitor. For me, success has really meant surpassing the goals I set for myself.

If I were talking to my teenage self right now, or any minority female teenager today, I'd tell her, "The most important thing in life is to seek the help you need to overcome any obstacles or challenges that you face. I'd also really get clear about your limits, but don't let them keep you from really shining and operating at your maximum potential—whether that's starting a business, changing the world, or going into a new, even rare business opportunity—one that hasn't even been envisioned yet."

Attitude, confidence, humility and the ability to be vulnerable will be key in your ability to map out your next step. In order to take actionable steps to make our ideas a reality, we definitely have to have an open attitude. More on that in the next chapter on flexibility, but, for now, just know that the help you require can come from anywhere, not just all the usual places you would expect. We've also hit on confidence already, but believing in and having faith and humility that you know what you're doing is key to taking action. By being vulnerable, I mean that you're able to go out, and seek the answers to your questions from resources you may not have considered before.

Because I've received help from so many people in my life, I try to serve others in everything I do. When I see someone struggling, I try to overcome that issue by focusing on how struggles can actually strengthen opportunities and make us better leaders. It's a great way to grow. I find it interesting and kind of unique to women that there are so many places where we do need to lead in response to a void. Kicking it in business isn't the end goal because there are so many other leading roles we need to fill—girl scout leader, cookie mom, snack shack coordinator, and Bible study leader to name a few. In a way, we take leadership home every single day.

FUTURE WOMAN MINDSET: Let struggles strengthen your opportunities so you grow through challenges. (Allison McGuire, Founder & CEO Walc)

I met Allison McGuire at the women's startup lab in Menlo Park and I believe she's a great example of this mindset. Four of us ladies in the program shared a room together for three weeks and Allison was one of my roommates. She came into the program with the Walc App which had recently gone through a rebranding. Previously the app was called SketchFactor which got a lot of heat from the press, especially Gawker, because it allowed users to mark "sketchy" experiences in urban locations so that urban walkers could avoid those areas.

Reviewers felt that the app catered to entitled (white) millennials who wanted to live in "trendy" parts of town but only wanted to walk on certain streets. Basically, the press called the app "tone deaf" and its founders racist. The intentions were good—to empower people to take good urban walks. However, only people with smartphones were so empowered—committing the sins of entitlement and privilege. Allison had to start her business again, ironically, from scratch by going back to the drawing board.

The rebranding of the Walc App has been really successful but put Allison through her paces with a great challenge of building a company twice. For Allison, walking is personal. She developed a love of walking after living in car-crazy LA. When she moved to Boston she needed an online tool to help her explore the city. A lover of travel and walking, she wanted to develop an app that would help other people who love to walk get around to see great places and have great walks in many cities. In the end, her frustrations became her inspirations and she finally developed Walc App, which uses landmarks to help people enjoy the great outdoors.

I admire that Allison built something from nothing twice. One of the biggest challenges professionally as a leader, and as an entrepreneur is the process of building something from nothing. For me, the hard part has been finding the right people who aligned with my goals and invested as much as I am to help the business expand. Even though I have to repeatedly explain an industry that doesn't exist and I've hit roadblock after roadblock, I don't let any struggle or challenge stop me from moving forward.

FUTURE WOMAN MINDSET: Always move forward. (Jewel Burks, Former Founder & CEO PartPic)

"I was surprised that there was this huge company that was having fails in their technology on a daily basis. I wanted to create a better way."

—Jewel Burks, Co-Founder of PartPic, an advocate for representation and access in the technology industry, former entrepreneur in residence for diversity markets at Google and currently a board member at Goodie Nation and the Harvard Debate Council Diversity Project, startup founder, mentor, and angel investor.

Jewel Burks is a great example of always moving forward. When she became an intern at Google, she felt like a fish out of water. She hailed from the South and needed to adapt to living in the mostly white male culture of Silicon Valley where they even served food in the Google cafeteria that she'd never heard of before. As difficult as she found the experience of moving and adjusting to another culture, in retrospect, she realized that the different social setting and environment provided a huge period of growth because it got her out of her comfort zone.

As I discovered in my experience, being out of my comfort zone defined and clarified my life's purpose. Depending on how you choose to respond to these kinds of situations, you'll either shrink back and give up on your dream, or you can use it to go to the next level and choose to expand and grow. Jewel chose the latter, having seen the value of hard work early in life.

She'd been exposed to entrepreneurship from a very early age because she came from a family of business owners. While growing up, she spent time with her mother in Nashville, watching her build up her own insurance agency and seeing firsthand the sacrifices her mom had to make in order for the business to be successful. She'd also spent time with her dad who ran convenience stores and laundromats which he'd inherited from Jewel's grandfather. As Jewel grew up, she'd help out at her dad's various enterprises working as a cashier and stocking refrigerators. As she worked, she developed the mindset at a young age that she could own a business too.

When an art teacher took her under her wing, Jewel got involved in painting and drawing, and, as a result, when she grew up, she thought she'd probably open up her own marketing agency, a good mixture of business and the art she enjoyed. But, after her internship at Google, she realized that she probably should have paid better attention in Calculus class because she enjoyed the world of technology, even though she wasn't really interested in math at all. Despite lacking the skills as a programmer, Jewel grew in her career and began to gravitate toward tech.

But she left Google in 2012 to move to Atlanta to be closer to her family when her grandma had been diagnosed with breast cancer. When she moved back, Jewel found work at a parts distribution company. Her job was in customer service and she received a lot of calls from angry customers who'd been shipped the wrong part. **Because she got sick of getting yelled at every day, she thought a lot about what she could do to change things.**

Lots of people didn't know what part they had that they needed to replace, so they would take a picture and send it in. But the parts distribution company didn't really have a place to put these photos or a way to identify the parts this way. In the midst of handling these problems at work, her grandfather even had a tractor breakdown and he wanted her to find a part for him, but she couldn't find it.

Basically she just kept experiencing this same issue over and over in different ways—**people needed parts and didn't know what they were or how to find them.** She wanted to find a way that would be easy for people to find parts just by people taking a picture of what they needed and that picture would be used to locate the part.

In solving her own problems, she was able to find a highly marketable solution. Although it took great persistence to keep moving forward, she had the necessary experience to come up with a solution because she was the solution provider every day at the company. She felt confident that she knew enough to discover a better way. In the search for a solution, Jewel decided to go deeper into the industry and thought about the potential monetization strategy.

When she analyzed the industry, she discovered that the current company was losing 33 million dollars every year due to erroneous shipments. These shipments cost the industry billions of dollars each year. Coupling this pain point with the search technology she learned at Google helped her formulate an idea to create an app called PartPic, a platform that helps users find items and replacement parts they need by taking a picture of them with their smartphones or tablets.

She felt there was a reason God took her from Google and placed her in a company where she wasn't really happy. Because of this, she could meet investors with full confidence in her pitch because of her unique experience with Google and the parts distribution company, both giving her unique insights into the industry she sought to help. But that confidence didn't last.

"My confidence changed when people were judging me on my appearance, that I was young and a black woman. People didn't really take me seriously. And so at that point I started second-guessing my idea and my experience."[22]

—Jewel Burks

Jason Chain, her cofounder, worked with her at Google. Around the time she left Google he started working at Shazam. She wanted PartPic to have the same easy feeling of clicking a button and getting an answer when searching for parts just like Shazam did with songs. She had a feeling that the technology would be similar for her app even though Shazam was audio and PartPic would be visual. Jason was one of the first people that Jewel shared her idea with and he agreed to let her know if the concept would be feasible. He went forward to work through the technical issues and soon discovered that her idea was feasible. This soon found Jewel and Jason recruiting Dr. Nashlie H. Sephus who ended up being the technical brains behind the app and also agreed to take a position of CTO.

"Formulating the right team to deliver the vision of replacing a part as easily as taking a picture had never been done before. And while creating the algorithms and prototypes for identifying and measuring replacement parts in a picture may sound easy, it required breakthrough technology, intense focus, and advanced technical acumen. You need people who share the same values, work ethic, and temperament, but who have diverse technical thoughts."[23]

—Dr. Nashlie H. Sephus, Applied Science Manager, Amazon Web Services; Founder, TheBeanPath.org

---

[22] http://behindthebrilliance.com/jewelburks/
[23] https://innotechtoday.com/nashlie-sephus/

There are two things Jewel advises when moving forward with a startup idea. First, really think about whether your business is one that needs to raise money through the VC process. It might be a better idea to bootstrap—the practice of relying on your own investments and capital to operate and expand your business with the cash that comes in from the first sales. Not every startup needs seed money to be successful. And secondly, if you do go the investor route, remember that investors are your boss and so are your customers.

There are many things to keep in mind if you do go the investor route. When you take on money, everything's great when all's well, but when things get hard, you need to know how your investors will react. For example, will they have your back when there's an acquisition deal on the table? Temperament and personality are important and often overlooked in the quest to come up with capital. It's all about getting the right fit for the culture of the business you hope to found. During Jewel's tenure as cofounder of PartPic, the company raised more than $2 million in funding.

Jewel always knew that when the time was right, she'd sell the company instead of going the IPO route. But the opportunity to sell came her way much sooner than she expected. She decided to sell because she thought that her original vision of the company would be better served by Amazon then going it on her own. In the end, Jewel Burks, and her cofounder Jason Crain, made a successful exit in 2016.

Jewel ended up playing in two white, male-dominated industries—the world of VC funding, and trying to attract customers in the industrial parts distribution world. She summed up this experience by saying, "There were lots of awkward moments. Any eye contact and answers given in these meetings were always directed to Jason. Of course, women always deal with this kind of thing. And this put a wall around me. I've since heard that back then, I had a reputation for being kind of hard or stone-faced. But I was really serious about what I was doing, and I wanted people to know that. But, for me, I was just so focused and I wanted to have people take me seriously. I wanted people to know that I had something worthwhile." [24]

I was given a head's up into the mindset of always moving forward when I cultivated an advisor named Geetha Rao, who I actually met after completing a female startup incubator in the Bay Area. She was recommended by one of her male colleagues who was a professor of Asian American Studies at Stanford University and one of the advisors in the incubator. He thought because of Geetha's background, she would be a good fit for me. When we initially talked on the phone we instantly clicked with one another.

It's interesting because she was a co-founder of a healthcare company which she cofounded with another female in Silicon Valley around ten years before I met her, way before blockchain even existed. During our conversations, she mentioned that she and her cofounder had a hard time gaining the confidence of VCs, as they were minority female entrepreneurs in the healthcare space at the time. Not only is this alarming from the standpoint of diversity and inclusion, it's even more unbelievable because she knew most investors she approached and even consulted for them.

This seems crazy because it is. Geetha is a Stanford and MIT graduate. One would think that anyone with those credentials would have investor confidence, no matter what gender or color of their skin. As a result, Geetha and her cofounder ended up dissolving the company because they were prompted to believe they were just too early in the space.

---

[24] http://behindthebrilliance.com/jewelburks/

When I listened to her story, I gained an insight into the insular mentality I'd have to deal with. This served as a cautionary tale for me, of course. I think her experience really made her want to advise me because I was a minority female entrepreneur in the healthcare space and she too lived a similar experience. Her mentorship was a huge factor for me going forward. As it turned out, I would meet up against this same bias time and time again. She did do one very valuable thing for me—she armed me and gave me the insights and tools I'd need to respond to what would come. Knowing how to respond to the inevitable setbacks and challenges as the founder of a startup is something Jewel Burks also recommended to new founders when going to bat with VCs.

Through the process of making my entrepreneurial dream come true, I learned that I can't do anything about the obvious prejudice that I would encounter, so I focused on all the things I did have control over. Geetha helped me a lot with my presentation and she was also willing to help me make great connections within the industry. Her introductions enabled me to get my foot in the door at places that would have taken me years to cultivate on my own. She also tooted my success to investors who more or less wouldn't have ever seen me come across their table.

FUTURE WOMAN MINDSET: Do everything you can do to master everything that is under your control. (Melissa Hanna, Cofounder & CEO Mahmee)

"One of the challenges underrepresented founders, like myself, are facing today is we don't have the typical backgrounds compared with the previous generation of founders in Silicon Valley. We don't fit into the San Francisco, Palo Alto white boys' club."[25]

—Melissa Hanna, co-founder of Mahmee, a Los Angeles-based prenatal and postpartum care management platform that looks to increase positive health outcomes for moms and babies.

Melissa is a great example of practicing this mindset with her belief that if you put in 200% of your efforts into your project, you've done everything you can. Unfortunately, even when people of color do so, Silicon Valley investors only give 0.0006% of capital to Black women. Not only that, but Melissa is trying to change the culture where meetings like hers devolved into investors endlessly questioning her background and credentials.

The idea behind Mahmee came to her in Los Angeles where she and her mom noticed a huge disparity between the networks of independent maternity care professionals who aren't doctors, such as nutritionists and lactation consultants, and large healthcare providers.

She was willing to do what it took for funding by going to meeting after meeting. But after one experience when an investor tried to delegitimize her, she got thrown off her game. He claimed that her law degree was a fraud because he'd never heard of the private law school in LA where she received her degree on full scholarship. So this distraction made it difficult for her to continue to pitch to the others seated around the table who actually didn't come to her rescue at all while he berated her.

---

[25] https://www.businessinsider.com/mahmee-founder-calls-on-silicon-valley-investors-to-be-more-courageous-2019-2

In response, Hanna is asking that investors have some courage to increase their investment in minority women. With more money going into establishing a greater presence for minorities in tech through organizations like Black Girls Code and Google's Women Techmakers, she hopes that the old guard of Silicon Valley will sit up and take notice. She's quick to point out that, "Meetings aren't funding. People take meetings all day; they don't write a check." Ultimately the people who are giving lip service to supporting diversity and inclusion need to act in concrete ways to make them happen.

But she didn't have to wait long to get more than lip service. She raised 3 million dollars in funding from Serena Williams, Mark Cuban, and Arlan Hamilton. On the financing round, Melissa had this to say, "Along the way, there were so many people that thought this should have been a charity project and a nonprofit organization and did not see the maternal and infant healthcare industry for what it is, which is a multi-billion-dollar market," Hanna said. "It's so gratifying to have these folks around the table with us now, like Arlan and Serena and Mark, who really get it and also want to see a big return on their investment and believe that's possible."

In my own experience over a period of eighteen months, I had reached out to more than 500 VCs in order to get funding for Patientory, and they all said no. I sat in on lots of the types of meetings Melissa talks about. The idea that I was entering the space too early became a common thread of rejection from investors. That space being the streamlining and securing of health data transmission processes to create better transparency for consumers, make doctors' jobs easier, and keep data more secure using blockchain technology. They also felt that I didn't really have an understanding of the scope of what I proposed. They felt all these things, even after I had won several pitch competitions, where one paid out a $10,000 prize. I was happy for every dollar, of course, but I would need many millions more to get Patientory off the ground.

Sure, at this point I could have given up. But I kept on going. I didn't even really know what to do to move forward or what my next steps would be, but when you want something bad enough and keep looking for opportunities, things fall into place. As the Bible says, "seek and you shall find." I'll let you know the rest of the story in the next chapter.

Everyone's is on a journey, but the minority journey is different, as you can see from all of the spectacular examples of minority and mindset listed above. And if you add the word blockchain to that journey, it's really different. It can make some things, like raising a first round of financing and questions of confidence, so much more difficult. But this just scratches the surface. Being a minority can add a level of complexity and nuance to every challenge. Mostly, things that you'd never anticipate will blindside you and you'll need to get over them. For me, one of the key issues involved financing. I would have to seek out another way to launch Patientory besides traditional VC funding.

It seems fair to say that as minority women, sometimes, we're doing everything that everyone else is doing, but with our hands tied behind our backs. As you can see, even when I found connections that were supposed to be sympathetic to my cause, things didn't go as I might have expected. And that kind of disappointment can make you lose hope. **But, I'm here to tell you there is hope. And it's usually one conversation away from your last disappointment.**

I've also discovered on my entrepreneurial path that everything boils down to integrity—knowing who you are and not being easily swayed. It's about following that gut feeling and slowing down enough to pay attention to that voice inside your head. I realize that this kind of advice is given often, but I state it here again for you to consider because I've found that this little voice inside can come in handy in ways I never anticipated. I had to learn to listen to my gut at a young age.

I had a real-life lesson in how to not let other people define me. And I also developed a mindset of responding and not reacting to the things that were done and said around me. It made me strong in ways I probably didn't understand at the time and would come in handy as I became an entrepreneur. And I guess that's when I started to take after my dad, who is a man of very few words. I think I've adopted his quietness as part of my mindset too.

My mother taught me some of the best lessons I received about mindset. Her favorite line is, "Common sense isn't sold in a shop." A person can't buy it. They either have it or they don't. She was very tough and sometimes harsh but only because she wanted me to think about my actions. She wanted me to be aware of the choices I made. She definitely pushed us kids to figure out who we were and to be problem solvers so we would be equipped and prepared for whatever came our way in life.

Sonia is my mom's name, and she was famous among my friends. As a matter of fact, when I had asked kids to come over, friends and their parents would joke about it and say, "Oh, you're going to 'Sonia's Bootcamp.'" Everyone in town knew she was very strict with us. But you know, while my older sister and I grew up, we never really had an issue with her strictness. And now that we look back, we realize that if she hadn't given us tough love, we wouldn't really appreciate where we are today. The discipline she instilled in us led to good self-discipline and great self-awareness.

There was also this quality of choice that she wanted us to understand. She let us enjoy the consequences of our choices. So she didn't step in to save us. She definitely wasn't the mom who would bring your lunch to school if you forgot it at home. Although nice and supportive, she held a tighter rein on us than most of the other kids in the neighborhood.

FUTURE WOMAN MINDSET: Common sense isn't sold in a shop. (Morgan Debaun, Co-Founder & CEO Blavity)

Morgan Debaun is a fantastic example of this kind of common sense. She founded a company called Blavity—a media company and platform for Black culture focusing on Black Millennials and they incorporate lifestyle brands like Travel Noir that also cater to Black culture. She founded the company in 2014 but never intended to found a media company. It all began in college when she and her friends sat around the lunch table talking about everything from politics to pop culture. They met at the same time every day and gravitated toward the same discussions. So she decided to mashup their sensibilities into Blavity, a word that reflects what she serves her readers—a place that gravitates toward discussions about Black culture. She has said that media isn't a great opportunity right now because the ad revenue is decreasing. When she first started, she didn't want to be in the world of media. She simply wanted to create an online space for Black Millennials to share their stories.

Her entrepreneurial journey began in Silicon Valley as she became immersed in the tech culture there, but she didn't feel like she could be herself. The idea for Blavity became solidified when she was living in San Francisco and found out that her hometown in St. Louis was on fire. During that tumultuous time, it was extremely difficult to find a lens that reported on the events relevant to her community. She felt frustrated that she couldn't find any pertinent information online even as the fire grew.

That's when the idea was born to take the information from Black people, like their phone numbers, and disseminate this information to other Black people who cared and trusted them to report on the important issues going on in the community. Fifty percent of the stories on Blavity are user-generated with editors who review and help vet them and create the article headlines. She also wanted to cover the rich diversity in blackness and foster a way for her demographic to have honest dialogue about hotbed issues. During the process, she discovered a need to work with content creators because they needed to cover big stories. She wanted and needed greater resources to cover certain stories responsibly, and that's why she eventually raised funding for them.

So she fought a few uphill battles to get her platform. One battle was how she needed to serve a section of the population that had been essentially left out of legacy media, and the second one involved building and growing a media company at a time when the industry was contracting. She decided to bootstrap her company because she wanted to create something of value that people trusted, and she thought once she had built something that people loved, she'd find an authentic way to speak to lifestyle issues and give a holistic experience for her readers.

In my opinion, nothing is more important than solidifying your entrepreneurial mindset when starting out. Getting clarity on what and how you'll move forward when challenges present themselves is key. If you take your cue from these extraordinary Future Women, you can find a way through the difficult issues outlined in this chapter, armed with all you need to take your startup to the next level. One of the keys to developing this winning mindset will be your flexibility and exercising this muscle in ways you never thought possible. Just how to go about looking at challenges and struggles in new ways is one of the many ideas explored in the next chapter.

FLEXIBILITY

"Stay flexible — change is the constant that keeps us on our toes."
—Chrissa McFarlane

I gained my first lesson in what flexibility really means while growing up. My mom bought her first house in Jamaica by the age of 30. She worked as an elementary teacher there and my dad worked at a bank. My parents had a comfortable life in Jamaica, but decided to move to America because they thought that they would find a better life here and get a great education for their kids. But they couldn't afford to move all of us at the same time, so they moved to New York with my older sister who's seven years older than me. I believe that they left me in the care of my grandmother in Jamaica because they had no other choice. The reality is that they needed to get jobs and work very hard, and I was just a baby, so they wouldn't be able to take care of me. I was born in December and they left after Christmas.

That was a decision my mom had to make. While we were separated, my dad would go back and forth between our community of Eltham Park in St. Catherine, Jamaica to New York City for around three years. Mom worked hard as a nanny because she couldn't get work as a teacher, and my dad similarly had to work in restaurants, as there were no jobs available for him in banking. They both worked hard to send money to my grandmother to take care of me. While it's a common theme in society for grandmothers to caretake young children, the world of remittance is uniquely that of immigrant families.

So, as you can imagine, I didn't have much of a relationship with my parents when I eventually moved to New York with them. Since I didn't really know my parents very well, I never called them Mom or Dad. Instead, I'd just say, "Hey you!" Getting dropped into a completely different culture with parents who looked vaguely familiar meant I had to adjust, as my parents had.

I watched my parents venture into starting businesses for themselves as I grew up. At that time, opportunities for minority women to become business owners just wasn't something I saw in my. I learned from a young age that if I didn't open a company myself, I wouldn't be able to materialize what I wanted to see in the business world—women having equal opportunities to harness their full potential without a glass ceiling.

I also absorbed the cost of what it means to make a dream come true. My parents went from living in a house of their own into a very tiny walk-up apartment. I would say that the whole experience was uncomfortable for them. I watched how they had to become self-sufficient, as they were now so far away from family and life-long friends who had supported them in Jamaica. Honestly, I believe that, looking back, knowing what they know today, they never would have moved. I saw firsthand that some dreams can turn into a growing experience.

Growing the dream

FUTURE WOMAN MINDSET: Consider your Version 1.0 and Version 2.0.

Just like my parents had to think flexibly when considering a move to New York City, my dream as an entrepreneur had a similar quality.

Sometimes, when you have a dream you have to accomplish it in steps, like my parents did with moving to a new country and then bringing me over at the right time, a version 1.0 and 2.0 approach. Similarly, I had to stay flexible when I chose to uproot from everyone and everything I knew in Atlanta to pursue an experience at the accelerator program in Boulder, CO. It was a program I was nominated to attend. But after creating a business plan for my company, I had a chance to fully understand the sophistication of my aspirations. I decided to make the company my life's work. One thing was certain; this new journey required assistance from the right people.

The idea to go with the accelerator program had all started with a hunch that there had to be another way. The feeling came from deep down inside of me as if something in my soul wanted to come out, but I'd kept it locked away for a really long time. I wrestled day and night with this vision of a better way, only to realize that this feeling never ends. Even four years later, I continue this perpetual cycle of refining my dreams, and with every passing minute, this same feeling helps me do the work needed to increase the success of the company.

This kind of passion caused me to send in an application late one night to potential accelerators who would be able to assist in my dream. I logged onto my computer and saw an email from the Boomtown Healthtech Accelerator for a request for an interview to be considered for their inaugural cohort program. I had done extensive research on Jose Vietez, the founder of Boomtown, and was amazed at the company's marketing and the many followers they were able to garner in such a short time.

So what's an accelerator, anyway?

FUTURE WOMAN MINDSET: Follow your heart and intuition.

An accelerator is basically a place for startups to get support in their early stage growth with educational, mentoring, and financing opportunities. They do this in a short time so that it shrinks the learning curve for launching a business from years to months. As you can imagine, this was an intense, exciting experience for everyone involved and provided rapid and immersive learning with the hope of accelerating the life cycle of innovative startups. The most powerful aspects of accelerators include a short, fixed term, that brings startups together with powerful cohorts and mentors, and a culmination in something called a "demo day," kind of like a graduation. Afterwards, the startup ideally will be more attractive to incubators, angel investors, and venture capitalists.

I was the sole founder of Patientory at the time, and the Boomtown Accelerator required that at least two people from the company be present on the interview call. I decided to invite my closest friend from undergraduate school, Natasha, to be the first employee of my company and represent us on the call. I let her know that if we got accepted, we would both have to move all the way across the country in less than three days. I had requested another gentleman who agreed to come on as CTO, but he wasn't able to commit to the risks and pressures of joining a young startup at that point in his life.

Three days after the call and our acceptance, Natasha and I moved from Hartford, Connecticut and Atlanta, Georgia respectively to Boulder, CO where we were the only women in the program made up of around forty men. The big move to Boulder was one of the many huge leaps of faith that I encountered on my journey to entrepreneurship. Natasha and I ended up moving into a room at the Millennium Hotel looking over the mountains in Boulder. For three months we shared a room and bathroom and grew close. But eventually, during the course of the challenging program, our relationship became strained, and we decided to go our separate ways. Like any startup, flexibility and execution is key. I managed to continue the program with two interns.

One of the hardest business decisions I had to make at that time in my career was to fire Natasha. This experience taught me the value of hiring slow and firing fast. While I felt Natasha's pain due to rejection, she also knew deep down inside that no matter how we considered ourselves sisters, Patientory wasn't her dream, and she had to find her own path. A month later, she ended up enrolling in a PhD program for criminal justice and we're still friends today.

> "Your time is limited, so don't waste it living someone else's life. Don't be trapped by dogma—which is living with the results of other people's thinking. Don't let the noise of others' opinions drown out your own inner voice. And most important, have the courage to follow your heart and intuition. They somehow already know what you truly want to become. Everything else is secondary."
>
> — Steve Jobs

Natasha and I learned the truth of what Steve Jobs said in a sort of painful way. But it also led to each of us living our own dreams. I basically call this following the breadcrumbs. And it's really good to make sure you know that they're there and what they look like for you. Because following someone else's breadcrumbs will never make you happy or fulfilled, and, most importantly, it will never lead you to your own path—the one the world needs you to travel.

The accelerator experience was a derisking one for me and a prestartup experience that equipped me for the long-term commitment to building Patientory. The accelerator gave me fuel. The goal was to really define my company and mission and to make it shatterproof. My work there did all of those things. I'd thought the accelerator experience would teach me how to get funding and help me find out all the answers I'd need to start my business. But the reality turned out very different, just as my parents had discovered when they moved to America. While the accelerator helped by connecting me to the community of startups, specifically in healthcare and with VCs who would also be interested in investing in my healthcare technology; I came back to Atlanta "low on runway," which is startup jargon for being short of operating capital, without any more answers than when I left.

As a result of taking so much time away and spending most of the capital I had raised in the accelerator program in Boulder, I had to move back in with my parents, and this felt like a giant step backwards. Sometimes, flexibility means doing things you never imagined, and trusting that it will reveal the next step that will get you that much closer.

I think what happened to me after the accelerator program really shows how being flexible can pay off. When I came back to Atlanta so fired up to take over the world and get all the financial backing I needed, I had a better idea of what my company could do, felt confident, and was ready to make my company happen. After a few months of really applying what I learned in the program, I had the right advisors, $100,000 in AWS (Amazon Web Services) credits, and mentors. But now I needed to find the financial backing to actually build a team to get the job done. I didn't really know what to do next.

So I asked around for people who knew about blockchain because, during the accelerator program, I realized this technology would be a driving force behind Patientory in disrupting the healthcare industry and overall population health management. I wanted to know more about who worked on blockchain locally in Atlanta. During my inquiries, a few people in town told me about Sean Wilkinson.

What can your peers teach you?

Initially I asked myself why I would talk to a 22-year-old. He was still in college. What did he know about companies or blockchain? The technology required extensive cryptography expertise at a PhD level. But I couldn't help but discover the work he did for people I knew in the blockchain world in Atlanta. Even so, I put off contacting him because that wasn't my main priority. My main priority was funding. I was talking to a lot of people at the time who were more experienced and I felt I had enough wisdom in that area and didn't think he would contribute anything new to the conversations I'd had.

But this didn't turn out to be true. Younger people contributed amazingly to my understanding. And this would be one of my main takeaways—that age doesn't matter when you're seeking help from people to gain a greater understanding. This was especially true in healthcare, which seems to only value people who've been steeped in the industry for decades. Knowledge is ageless.

The coworking space I worked at invested in him, and the coworking space's manager introduced us. They invested in him because he was financing for his company and the founders of the coworking space were Georgia Tech alums where he was a student. I soon discovered that he'd completed a token sale in 2015, before it was even called a token sale, and raised half a million dollars. Shortly afterwards,

Ethereum were one of the first ones to raise money in this way as well.

I remember my hesitation at the time. It intrigued me that he'd held a token sale before, but I didn't consider that arena my playing field because I saw token sales as a type of crowdfunding. I felt people wouldn't take Patientory seriously if I took a crowdfunding approach. However, things change quickly and this attitude of not considering token sales seriously is slowly becoming a thing of the past.

So I let all this information sit for about five months as I worked hard to make my own contacts with investors. And one day, when I was really desperate, I searched for his contact information which had been buried in my email and reached out to the boy genius. My email read something like, "Oh hey, nice to meet you; let's get on a call sometime."

We arranged to meet at his office at the Atlanta Tech Village, the third largest coworking space in the country. I and my two team members went to his office, and I thought the location of his office was so cool. The energy there really impressed me. As soon as I entered the inspiring place, I knew that I wanted to work there someday. Today, his office location is now my own.

In that meeting, he told me all about cryptocurrency, how he went about making his own cryptocurrency and how his team used cryptocurrency to fund the business. He was a young crypto adapter who gave me techniques I could use that would turn out to be the pulse of how my business would thrive and eventually led to the best way to raise capital for Patientory. He later came on as an advisor.

Cryptocurrency wasn't an area I expected to pursue so early in the company's journey. I had lots of reasons for this, but the main one came from constantly hearing that crowdfunding was looked down upon by VCs and techies. They also felt that there was rarely any crypto adoption in the mainstream markets. In my mind, crowdfunding wasn't as serious a method as raising cash the traditional way.

After doing more research, I observed that successful crowdfunding companies sold merchandise. So I actually stopped the young expert in the meeting and said, "No, I don't think you understand who we are. We're a healthcare company." And he politely assured me that crowdfunding was applicable for my company too with the right execution and use case for this new trusted economy. But, there was such a disconnect in my mind about what he suggested. Like healthcare and cryptocurrency couldn't possibly go together. What I didn't need was more skepticism in the space, seeing all the negative publicity surrounding bitcoin at the time.

Another reason why I didn't go for the idea right away was the Cap Table (short for capitalization table which lists everyone who owns a portion of the company by shares and percentage) that I would be announcing and the structure of the funding. In my opinion, capital raising in the form of crowdfunding would create too many stakeholders, meaning that the future stakeholder would be taking on undue risk because there were so many initial investors.

FUTURE WOMAN MINDSET: Stay open to opportunities that you don't expect.

My newly minted young advisor ended up introducing me to individuals in the crypto space who assisted him in his last sale. I really connected with one of them who lived in Gibraltar where they were headquartered. And my conversation with the Gibraltar connection about blockchain ended up changing the whole trajectory of my business. These connections enlightened me more on how to create my own cryptocurrency and getting it into the hands of people. Ironically, I had fallen in love with Gibraltar after living abroad in Spain. The rock of Gibraltar in ancient times was seen as the limit to the known world and served as Hercules pillars in Greek mythology.

If that conversation hadn't happened, we wouldn't be where we are today and providing a beacon of light to pave the way for execution of Patientory's transformative mission. **But understand that this one conversation didn't happen overnight. I had met over 300 people in the accelerator program, which led to the introduction that led to this conversation that would transform my business.**

It's kind of ironic actually when I look back because cryptocurrency was on the cutting edge of financing the way I hoped my business would be. Essentially, only around three or four companies had done what we were about to do. So I decided why not be a Guinea pig?

When I talked to the team in Gibraltar about my company, they instilled that confidence I needed to go ahead and try because they felt that Patientory needed to be out there in the ecosystem. They had mentioned they worked with some popular people in the space, including Gnosis, so I decided to give it a shot. And at that point, I figured, why not? Nothing else had worked. And as time went on, they became advisors for our cryptocurrency and a champion for the company. They worked with me to feel comfortable about running the whole funding process with them. Basically, we hosted a token sale similar to the ICO (Initial Coin Offering) in the cryptocurrency space. ICOs attracted more capital than all early stage Internet startups from traditional Venture Capital funds in June and July of 2017.[26]

---

[26] *Crowdfunding in crypto ecosystem.* blackmooncrypto.com. 2017.
https://news.blackmooncrypto.com/crowdfunding-in-crypto-ecosystem-

When all this information came my way, I actually had my foot out the door on the whole Patientory idea. I was in that place of coming to terms with how it was never going to happen. In the back of my mind, I thought, *well if this doesn't go anywhere in like two months, I'll have to shut it down and go back to grad school, I guess.* So, I applied to law school, and had taken my GMATs and looked at graduate programs all while my parents played devil's advocate and came down on me with all kinds of questions like, *Why are you doing all this? You went to an Ivy League school; why are you trying to start a company?*

Going all in

I had been all in, and it looked like I couldn't find my way out. I had one foot out the door on my dream, as I said, but that one foot inside knew that I hadn't come all this way to go nowhere. But, at that point in my life, I felt like a failure. And, instead of focusing on the future and what I could do next, I spent a lot of time asking myself what I did wrong. I mean, I'd been raised by Bootcamp Sonia to always support myself, so much so that at a very young age, I'd sell candy bars to open up a savings account for myself. I'd always found ways to make money, even when times were really tough. So why couldn't I figure it out now as an adult?

It was really difficult to have to financially rely on my parents during that time. Even though I would tell myself things like it's all about balance, and realize that other cultures don't have the stigma we do about moving home to live with our parents, moments like that really made me feel like my dream of owning my own business might not come true.

31b4818f0327. Accessed June 2019.

But, after coming out on the other side of this tough time, I've discovered that following a big dream is like driving a car in the middle of the darkest night. I want the high beams on, or at least a full moon so that I can see everything in front of me and know where to turn and prepare for what's down the road. I want exact directions. But accomplishing a big dream isn't like that at all. Heck, life isn't like that either. I really believe it's better not knowing because God (whatever your perception of Him) doesn't want us to see everything. In a way, when you set out to accomplish a dream, it's a sacred task. It's about trusting and having faith. It's knowing that He may have only lit up one small spot on the road, but the next one will illuminate in His perfect timing.

In short, lots of times, I invested in opportunities and tried to accomplish objectives that led to seemingly nowhere. However, if I hadn't explored some of these avenues, I wouldn't have found the road or even the conversation that would take me to a successful token sale.

How does flexibility play a part in creating more female entrepreneurs?

FUTURE WOMAN MINDSET: Have faith in yourself and your dream.

Sometimes, flexibility means doing things you never imagined, trusting that it will reveal the next step that will get you that much closer to accomplishing your dream. So, how does flexibility play a part in creating more female entrepreneurs? The big move to Boulder was one of the biggest leaps of faith I encountered on my journey to entrepreneurship. I needed to develop the courage to jump off a cliff (move and invest everything I had) to take what I call a "gut chance" in life. By living out my dream in this way, I got the opportunity to understand how to follow my own breadcrumbs. I think I was able to be so flexible because I'd had to develop ways to adapt at a very young age. And even after college, the firsthand entrepreneurial experience came with the realization that I wouldn't be a doctor. I adapted by trading my childhood dream to pursue a calling of deeper meaning that fulfills me every day in ways my original dream never could.

At times, being flexible made me afraid, and it might make you afraid too at times. But know that no good decision is made in fear. We have to feel the fear and act in spite of it and not be held hostage by its negativity and worry (usually about things that will never happen). At one point, I felt I had failed in life because I didn't pursue becoming a physician, which is what I had originally held myself accountable to accomplish. But a more important calling illuminated over time, and found me combining my passion for healthcare and my knowledge of technology in a way that surprised me (and a lot of the VCs who turned me down too). Ultimately, being flexible led me to a successful token sale of 7.2 million dollars, and you better believe the phone started ringing then. Everyone wanted in. And now it was up to me to pick and choose whom I wanted on my team—one of the most critical decisions any leader needs to make.

Keys to flexible thinking

I found one of the keys to this kind of flexible thinking is mental health. It's important to not fixate on issues in your business. Driving yourself crazy doesn't get you or the company anywhere. The only way that you'll make sure you're making the right decisions is by living a harmonious life. This doesn't mean that you don't work hard and make some sacrifices in your work-life balance. But it does mean that you're able to sustain good mental health so you make sure your decisions don't hurt you emotionally and financially.

FUTURE WOMAN MINDSET: Take care of your body, mind and spirit every day.

I've found meditation to be a key tool that helps me ground myself so I'm better able to cultivate the serenity needed to stay flexible in the most stressful of situations. I know that meditation and mindfulness gets a lot of lip service. It seems that every magazine I pick up these days has something to say about it. Trust me, I've tried everything to try to help me center and stay on track. In my opinion, meditation works because you can do it for as long as you feel comfortable and it's always beneficial. It's something I got good at over time. And as antsy as I was when I first started, I can't imagine a day without it now. I look forward to closing out the world for a while and breathing in my own experience in silence.

Another way I make sure to take care of my mental health is to do great self-care. You would think that someone who's trying to champion a better way to do healthcare in the world would be great at taking care of herself. Sadly, this isn't always the case. I used to work long hours and never took breaks during the day. But I've changed all that. Time is a precious thing so I've taken steps to make sure I schedule some down time. **Monday to Friday is solely dedicated to work goals but after 5 or 6, I wind down and do whatever I choose, whether that's going to a restaurant or checking out some new art exhibit. I call it unmapped time.** I've also begun a practice of taking the first week of the month to maintain my health like scheduling massages and chiropractic appointments.

I had the pleasure of learning a lot about time management from my dean at Cornell, Janice Turner. During the beginning of my Freshman year, I got sucked into the bad habit of going to dinner early at 5, as soon as dining halls opened to avoid lines. The time I saved when I should have been studying only found me hanging out with my friends and anyone who decided to join in on the conversation, which usually went on until around nine at night. We'd just talk about everything and I ended up spending leisure time studying. When I wasn't doing well in my chemistry class, my dean actually recommended that I attend a time management workshop. After putting into practice everything I learned at that workshop, time management has become second nature.

Whenever I slip up, I can hear Janice's voice. She just comes to me when I'm not managing my time well. For example, not too long ago, I had a lunch meeting with someone I met at a networking event and we'd scheduled an hour to get to know each other better. But when the lunch went over the hour, I knew that it was time to get going and get back to what I had to take care of that afternoon, as if an internal alarm started to go off. Now, I'm really careful with my time.

When a problem, such as my poor time management, arises, often, a solution is close by. In my case, I had someone who was willing to give me the exact resources I needed to manage my time better and succeed in school. I believe that if you stay open to the opportunities around you and engage the wisdom of the people who are available to help, you'll find the solutions you need.

FUTURE WOMAN MINDSET: When you need help, ask for it.

Great mental health means taking good care of your time and yourself each day. Every day, I ask myself: What do my body, mind, and spirit need? We often hear about the connection between our body, mind, and spirit being important to our overall health. I know that when they're all working in harmony, I'm better able to stay flexible to the disappointments, setbacks, and challenges that arise. I believe that when we stretch our body, mind, and spirit in new ways to achieve new levels of awareness, it's easy to withstand the pressures we face daily on the job because our ability to respond to life also becomes more flexible.

My awareness opened up the most when I had to deal with the consequences of hardship, for example, when I was bullied in my first startup job and faced multiple rejections later during my funding meetings. These were times when I had to have the mental toughness and flexibility to not go down the rabbit hole of the kind of black-and-white thinking that suggested that because some people treated me poorly, everyone would treat me this way and their bad behavior reflected on me somehow. Instead, I enjoyed developing the perspective after working very hard on my awareness and mental health, that those actions were a reflection of the people who behaved poorly and said more about them than it did about me or my ideas.

In short, these were the kinds of insights I gained after these lessons. Under extreme pressure, we can lose sight of certain boundaries, like being responsible for our own feelings. Really, it's about not taking anything personally and knowing that only you have the ability to make yourself feel, no one else—so responding instead of reacting is key.

FUTURE WOMAN MINDSET: Future Women need each other; cultivate a generosity of spirit together.

Another way to stay mentally strong is to always network and keep current on trends in and outside of your business. Everything you can do to keep your mind stimulated and on track with your goals and values will make you sharper, better able to make decisions, and a lot less vulnerable to frustration and disappointment. Constantly networking is a way of building a tribe of people to connect with that will help get you through the tough times. The wisdom they've cultivated would otherwise take you years to cultivate on your own. I do this by attending networking events, but I also stay plugged in digitally with certain websites and podcasts I read and listen to that keep me vibrating high and focused on what I need to accomplish in that season. For female entrepreneurs, there are many networking groups online like The Frontrunners League and Blockchain Ladies: The Network, and you can usually find other entrepreneurial groups in your area that are available to keep you meeting new people whom you can learn from and inspire.

Here are a few of past and present go-tos I've used to help keep me focused on my goals and flexible in my mindset. An app that I've recently enjoyed listening to is called *Living With Power*. I listen to this daily and use it to help me stay in balance and inform my perspective. It has an inspirational message and give daily tips to stay grounded in hope. It's fun too because you can share it with friends on social media and it even has a customizable journal. A podcast that I've loved in the past is called *Two Dope Queens*, in which two minority Millennials just talk about everything. It's kind of a cool mixture of romance, culture, and everything in between through the lens of two minority women. Other media I visit include Travel Junkie Diary (http://traveljunkie diary.com) and Travel Noir (https://legacy.travelnoire.com/).

I also take inspiration from the networking I did at my accelerator experience. While I took part, a team of people from India there gave me a great lesson in flexibility. Obviously, we all had our own sacrifices we had to make in order to take part in the intensive three-month program. But the team from India had many more. They had to fly all the way to America and apply for the appropriate Visa to enter the country for the program. But when they arrived, they didn't have a place to stay. Since they didn't know anyone in Boulder, CO they actually needed to sleep at the accelerator for a while until they found some accommodations. Most of them also had families and children they had to be separated from during the intense program. Their flexibility under pressure inspired me. The sacrifice and passion they had to invest in their dream by traveling across the world and the competence they had in their business life impressed me beyond measure. When they arrived, they hit the ground running, even though they were on the other side of the world with nowhere to stay.

Staying resilient

As I reflected on the kinds of flexibility required by Future Women, I really saw the parallels to what doctors say about the health benefits of flexibility and the advice given in healthcare:

"Better flexibility may:

- Improve your performance in physical activities
- Decrease your risk of injuries
- Help your joints move through their full range of motion
- Enable your muscles to work most effectively

Stretching also increases blood flow to the muscle. You may learn to enjoy the ritual of stretching before or after hitting the trail, ballet floor, or soccer field." —The Mayo Clinic

This could be rewritten in my opinion to become a kind of Future Woman flexibility mantra to remind us how to protect ourselves on our entrepreneurial journeys. Similarly to well-stretched muscles, the better you are able to stay flexible in your mindset, the better you'll perform on the entrepreneurial playing field.

In my experience, better flexibility in our mindset will:

- Improve your ability to follow your heart and intuition
- Decrease your chances of missing opportunities that you don't expect
- Help you have faith in yourself and your dreams
- Encourage taking care of your body, mind, and spirit every day
- Give you the courage to ask for help when you need it
- Foster a generosity of spirit that encourages networking and lifting each other up

When you put these flexibility mindsets into practice, your entrepreneurial performance will improve because you'll decrease your risk of making poor decisions, as you've allowed yourself the space to gain perspective and bring balance into your life. One of the key factors that helps ground and center us are the informed choices we make that are in line with our values. This is one of the most crucial decisions you'll have to make in business.

FINANCIAL EMPOWERMENT

"Solutions will arise with patience, effort and perseverance."
—Chrissa McFarlane

Because this mindset is so important, I've dedicated a chapter to helping you get clear about how to be and stay financially empowered on your entrepreneurial journey. And I think the best way to harness your financial empowerment is to stay focused on your professional goals at all times, even when crazy comes to town. And crazy will; trust me.

I had hundreds of meetings with VCs. They loved my idea for my company, but I didn't gain any traction. Pretty much every meeting had some version of this script:

I'd wow them with my idea, and then?

"Oh, we love this… but we don't have an appetite for investing at this time," said over 300 VCs.

I was like, really?

But as soon as I received a large funding round, everyone started to court me and wanted in fast. In my opinion, any opportunity worth investing in, is worth putting in an early investment. The same men who didn't have the time of day for me were now asking me out to dinner. My thoughts on the other end of the phone or keyboard? *Where were you two years ago, when I actually needed funding and you blew me off when we were supposed to have that meeting?*

But during that time of rejection, I had to stay focused on what I could do to move the process forward. I couldn't live in what opportunities didn't exist, instead I had to think positively and creatively to see a solution when it presented itself. During the crowdfunding period, people became attracted to the idea of the company based on its emotional appeal to real issues people had to face in their healthcare. The reality of the problem we were solving made financial sense in a way that left VCs in the dust and garnered much more attention than they'd imagined.

In contrast, large companies like Amazon and Facebook got their start because the old guard bet on them. But I'm here to ask the question, "Who in Silicon Valley ever bet on a minority woman?" Not many did. As I said earlier in the book, the startup funding statistics are alarming for minority women.

Let's change that statistic.

How to become financially empowered

One of the ways we can change the future is by becoming financially empowered. The best way we can become more powerful as a financial force in the future is by taking a peek at our financial pasts to understand where our experience was and where it's headed. For instance, everyone has ingrained from an early age a financial compass that they've received from a variety of people in their lives—parents, friends, and teachers. I received many financial empowerment lessons while growing up from all of these perspectives. When my family immigrated, beyond the struggle of what they had to leave behind in Jamaica, they also struggled to thrive in a new society.

I could tell something heavy weighed on their hearts, although they never mentioned anything to me directly. They saw the dangers my sister and I were exposed to every day in our neighborhood. We grew up in the North Bronx, which was predominantly first-generation immigrants, mostly from the Caribbean. The neighborhood wasn't a bad environment, but my parents saw what kinds of things the other kids in the neighborhood got into and knew where those dangerous behaviors would lead. So, they taught us the lessons of hard work and frugality.

I specifically remember my mom waking up every morning at dawn to make our breakfasts and our lunches. Sometimes, my sister and I wondered why we couldn't buy our lunches like other kids who received allowances from their parents. But mom wouldn't hear of it. Over time, blending in and not doing what the rest of the kids did became difficult, especially in high school. But my mother stood firm and continued making our breakfasts and lunches until the day I graduated from high school and even made some for my classmates. That was the level of her dedication.

And for some reason, her dedication in making my breakfast and lunch every day also contributed to fueling my ambitions. Immigrant kids have a unique experience because they usually see their parents arriving and adapting to a strange new land where they have to struggle sometimes. I didn't want to face those same circumstances, and I wanted to make my parents proud with my independence. I think this gave me my first lesson in financial empowerment—I wanted to be able to be in control of my finances instead of having my finances dictate the choices I'd have to make in life.

FUTURE WOMAN MINDSET: Be in control of your finances instead of having your finances dictate the choices you have to make in life.

During college, I went to school on a scholarship. This meant that I didn't need to participate in a work-study as a provision of keeping my scholarship, which required students to work a minimum of twenty hours per week on campus doing things like serving food and helping in the student union. However, I decided to go ahead and find a job anyway, not only for the potential experience I might gain that could inform my future career but also because of the financial independence it would it provide.

I didn't want to rely on my parents for my spending money. Even though they generously provided some resources for me, I knew that this provision would be a burden on them, and I wanted to be in control of my finances instead of having my finances dictate my choices. So I got a job at a hospital and had an early exposure to the healthcare industry before I graduated.

But the job didn't just fall in my lap. I had to do my homework to get the position. My search for opportunities began on the school website where I saw a list of jobs, and I reached out to the Principal Investigator of a federal laboratory where I ended up working for two years. Once the graduate student I worked with defended her dissertation and graduated, I went on to create and implement a program with the Executive Director of a nonprofit who ran multiple initiatives with the local hospital.

It all seemed serendipitous. The Executive Director asked for a meeting that summer back on the hill before classes started and I decided to oblige. Once we met, she created a role for me at the nonprofit called the Mental Health Association of Tompkins County just outside of Cornell where I went to school. I became their healthcare outreach person. Come to think of it, that's essentially what I am now at Patientory, advocating for healthcare in a digital way. **My job at MHA** of Tompkins Country was one of the biggest financially empowering moments of my life because the Executive Director created a position just for me, which would help keep me in better control of my finances and inform my career.

This was a part-time job and involved writing grants for the program and going to the hospital to meet with adolescent patients and the attending physicians where I ran roundtables, did community outreach, and helped with programming. I remember working there one Thanksgiving where we all helped to serve dinner to the patients, and this helped me to discover my value of being in service to others. **The job that they created for me in college really launched me into the nonprofit healthcare world in ways I would never have experienced if I hadn't searched for the opportunity and made financial empowerment a priority.**

After I got the job, most of my friends who were also looking to get into medicine told me that they thought my position sounded like an amazing opportunity and they asked me to get them a job there too. This also made me feel financially empowered because jobs don't just happen. I realized that control of my finances was something that I needed to prioritize and strive for because I'd have to make my own opportunities. My financial empowerment would involve prioritizing, seeking, and finding the right opportunity and becoming clear about my financial objectives.

FUTURE WOMAN MINDSET: Prioritize seeking and finding the right opportunity, and become clear about financial objectives.

Although my choice to take on a job, even though it wasn't a stipulation of my scholarship might be surprising, I'd been equally surprised by the choices of some of my fellow students. For instance, I was shocked to discover that some of my friends, whose parents were doctors, had to work and they didn't have a choice. I figured those students would have had some kind of golden ticket that would alleviate them from worrying about their finances. I thought they would have been able to just go to school without having to work.

That experience made me realize that even people I thought would be in control of their finances aren't sometimes. I also experienced plenty of other people I knew who modeled some irresponsible behavior around their finances as they got into debt even though their parents paid for college. What happened to them and their life choices in the aftermath of bankruptcy also helped to shape my ideas about how to become financially empowered. During my college years, I realized that financial empowerment meant having control over financial situations. This leads to financial freedom, which allows people more flexibility in their lifestyle and work-life balance.

FUTURE WOMAN MINDSET: Financial empowerment leads to financial freedom which allows people more flexibility in their lifestyle and work-life balance.

My job in college also made me feel empowered because I was in a position of authority. I helped patients and liaised with the doctors and nurses who took care of them. So I realized that while exploring financial empowerment in my own life, I also helped empower other people to live their best lives too.

FUTURE WOMAN MINDSET: Financial empowerment leads to empowering others on their journey.

I've experienced a tie to financial empowerment and empowering others over the course of my life. I find empowering other people on their journey is a real calling and one of the greatest benefits of financial empowerment. I believe that values bring clarity and intention to financial empowerment. Serving others and commitment are two values that help guide my financial empowerment choices. Whether lifting each other up with opportunities at companies that we found or serving a Thanksgiving turkey dinner to people in need, Future Women give back and pay it forward. More about this kind of lifting up in the chapter called *Transformation*.

FUTURE WOMAN MINDSET: Future Women give back and pay it forward.

Beyond paying my cell phone bill, which my parents and I decided would be my responsibility, I made decisions about how to save and spend the money I earned. Because of this freedom, I was able to take part in activities that I would have missed if I hadn't been working. I made it a priority to save 10% of my money after my 10% tithe and found this to be a great financial discipline because I paid God first and me second.

Sure, it was fun to be able to afford to go out for Sushi on a Friday night, but I also saved up for things like taking a medical mission trip to Honduras in Central America. It was my first time outside of America other than Jamaica, so I had been very excited to travel to a new country in a new part of the world. With the help of my savings and other grants, I made my dream of helping others come true. This was another big moment of financial empowerment in my life. And when I lived through the experience, it made me realize that financial empowerment allows me to dream big, much bigger than if I didn't feel in control of my financial destiny.

FUTURE WOMAN MINDSET: Financial empowerment allows you to dream big.

Getting myself to Honduras helped me understand the importance of financial independence in my life. For example, I didn't have to beg my parents to go. I simply decided and made it happen. My mom instilled this independent nature and that probably came from her immigrant experience of having to start life over in a new country with no family or contacts. So I've had this philosophy that I'm basically the creator of my own experience, including what kind of opportunities I want to bring into my life and where I want to have those experiences.

My mom wasn't happy about me traveling to Central America because she feared that something might happen to me. But, in the end, she got over her fear and supported my experience there.

FUTURE WOMAN MINDSET: You are basically the creator of your own experience including what kind of opportunities you want to create and where you want to have those experiences.

I had saved quite a bit of money over time and had the great good fortune to use it to help fund my applications for grad school. Obtaining advanced degrees is also another way that I built my independence. Overtime, the discipline of saving also allows for flexibility in risk taking, such a starting a new endeavor. I was able to jump off a cliff at my startup and bootstrap prior to joining an accelerator program. I learned that having resources at key times in my life proved useful in the formation of my career as the Founder and CEO at Patientory.

FUTURE WOMAN MINDSET: Having resources at key times in my life proved useful in the formation of my career.

Financial empowerment resources

I've thought a lot about what needs to take place for successful minority entrepreneurship in light of where I've been and what I've been able to accomplish so far. I feel financial empowerment really has to occur before any risk is taken in the world of business. For those entering university, deciding to earn a college degree is one of the biggest investments and financial empowerment decisions you can make in life.

In books like *Think and Grow Rich*, by Napoleon Hill, plans for achieving success and financial peace are laid out to help you accomplish this kind of financial empowerment and financial freedom mindset. Because of my experience reading Napoleon Hill's ideas on abundance and financial acuity, I keep a list in the Notes App on my iPhone called "Life Lessons." They're organized into the four categories Napoleon Hill outlines in his book: management of cash flow, management of systems, marketing and sales, and management of people. **This list is where I come up with ideas, plans, and strategies for how I'm going to obtain money, how money comes in, and what to do with money when it does come in.** It keeps my financial life front and center. I like to use my notes there to help me be a good steward of my money and that involves the planning process.

FUTURE WOMAN MINDSET: Being a good steward of your money involves the planning process.

A big part of the planning process and financial empowerment is charting a course for success. If you doubt you have the necessary skills to succeed in a certain field, a training course or educational program is most likely the best investment toward financial empowerment. Although in order to get those skills, most of the time, you'll need to contribute resources such as capital or time. For instance, I had to feel financially empowered (even at moments of major disempowerment) to risk paying all the money I had raised and saved at the time to enter the Boomtown Healthtech Accelerator program, which turned out to be a total game changer.

Accelerator programs are valuable, but only if they're inclusive. Without my experience at the inclusive Boomtown Accelerator, I probably wouldn't have moved forward and started to put some of the missing puzzle pieces of my business together so rapidly. I think we have to look at our experience wherever we are on our journey of financial empowerment, and be flexible enough to stay open to new ways that might help move us forward. I believe the biggest key to moving forward toward financial empowerment lies in acceptance. The acceptance of where we are now, instead of beating ourselves up over it, allows us to recognize and take advantage of opportunities that would certainly pass us by otherwise. Because I didn't dwell on what wasn't coming my way, I was better able to recognize and take part in the opportunity that allowed me to collaborate with a cohort that transformed my company.

FUTURE WOMAN MINDSET: The acceptance of where you are now, instead of beating yourself up over it, allows for you to recognize and take advantage of opportunities that would certainly pass you by otherwise.

How did I end up making that connection? Well, it didn't appear out of the blue. I had to stay aware and focused on what I wanted to accomplish in my career and connect my own dots. Since I needed help starting my company, I listed my idea for my company on a site for accelerators, where new founders can seek connections—kind of like startup exchange websites. Boomtown Accelerator had reached out to me when they saw I had applied as part of their outreach. My analytical inclination proved invaluable in the legwork required to put me and Patientory out there and particularly helped as I looked for connections for startups in the healthcare space. Ingenuity brought on by lots of closed doors helped me become empowered in ways I never would've acquired had the VC route been available.

The minority experience in the VC world is difficult in ways that are complex, yet very clear. In the healthcare space, when I advocated for a company that would be using blockchain to revolutionize the healthcare industry worldwide, VCs didn't have a lot of success stories to research with the hopes of seeing where previous founders have been successful in the space. I was essentially the architect of a new space, so this made my conversation much harder.

However, it's not like I was talking about a unicorn. In conversation after conversation, when VCs would talk about their low level of confidence in me because I'd been untried in a space akin to the healthcare equivalent of putting a man on the moon, part of me laughed. You see, in Silicon Valley, VCs regularly take risks on untried founders, some in their late teens, with no background in the business they desire to create. Do these young men (mostly) jump through MIT, Harvard, and Stanford hoops only for VCs to give them a vote of no confidence and no money? No, these guys get their financing with ideas that have been hatched in their dorm room.

FUTURE WOMAN MINDSET: Comparison doesn't serve us. Breaking the mold does.

I couldn't help but wonder as the doors continued to close, *why is this happening now?*

I just didn't get it. The whole thing seemed so unfair and totally out of pace with the way the world was moving outside of the United States. Honestly, I spent a lot of time scratching my head trying to come up with reasons why. Obviously, as in most industries, this kind of rubber hits the road stuff isn't taught in school. And, as in a lot of other industries, I felt I had met up with an old boys' club that, unfortunately, mirrors the opportunities in our country too.

How do you stay empowered when the deck is stacked against you?

Founding my own company didn't come easy. At times, I thought about just dropping the whole thing. I faced so many obstacles. But what I noticed in the fullness of time is that when a setback of one degree or another occurred, I'd always find the perfect way through.

Was it what I expected or how I envisioned developing my company? Most of the time, the forks in the road surprised me. But if I hadn't had the core feeling of empowerment, I'm convinced that I wouldn't have been aware and able to see the opportunities that presented themselves, which ended up launching Patientory.

I've learned how to cultivate this kind of empowerment in the wake of the odds by developing connections that kept me and my company strong. I didn't shrink back from the process. I leaned into the process, and when I did, I discovered that the startup ecosystem is key. A rapport is built in the ecosystem unique among any other networking opportunity. It's so important to have advisors who have a heart for helping to build your company the way you imagine. Accelerators are definitely a part of that special group of advisors who helped to reinforce my company's mission. I'm also part of women startup groups, and women in blockchain groups, which help me to periodically reenergize and encourage me to actually accomplish my goals.

FUTURE WOMAN MINDSET: Have advisors with a heart for helping you build a company the way you imagine.

Of all the times in my life, I probably felt the most financially empowered during the crowdfunding token sale event. The process became a validation of my company because so many people were really seeing the viability and value of the business model, something I'd begun to doubt in the wake of the massive rejections I faced from VCs. It was an experience that brought to mind what I love about cryptocurrency: it's colorblind, doesn't care about your gender, and reaches around the world.

However, just because you're empowered doesn't mean that you won't run into bumps in the road. In the implementation of the token sale, I was constantly coached from legal regarding the SEC which didn't feel very empowering at all. But I believe the forces are changing. We need to have a conversation about wealth in this country. The conversation needs to be about how and who gets to define what wealth means. Hopefully, we can have some transformation on how we classify the wealthy in the coming years in America.

I'd like to start the conversation by putting into question the hundred-year-old rules that are still on the books about who is able to become an accredited investor. For example, in my case, the SEC has determined that only people with a minimum net worth of $200,000 can become accredited investors. This policy leaves investment open to only people in certain income brackets, leaving out many potential investors and decreases the investment pool. This results in investors, venture capital firms, and finance companies that aren't reflective of our diverse culture, so minorities are very often left out of the picture. With this current structure, a person has to be wealthy to get wealthy.

While creative workarounds exist, they are fraught with their own hassles. Today startups can raise capital through security token offerings, as opposed to the untried token sales of 2017. There also now exists new regulations when it comes to crowdfunding. Regulation D 506(b) and 506(c) now offers startups the limited offer and sale of securities, which doesn't require registration under the Securities Act of 1933.

But, swimming against the tide by using the token sale instead of going the traditional VC route meant I had to exclude American investors due to the gray areas that existed in the United States regarding cryptocurrency. Because of our current laws, I left America to find support elsewhere.

This experience turned out to be both positive and negative, which is expected for your startup journey. Without these experiences and challenges and learning I wouldn't have received the opportunities for my company to expand and thrive. Financially empowerment for me meant I had to stay flexible and seek out new connections that opened up ways I might not have originally considered. This was exactly what the Gibraltar team's suggestion did for me.

FUTURE WOMAN MINDSET: Stay flexible and seek out new connections that open up ways you might not have originally considered.

Breaking down the token sale

So let's break down what the token sale actually meant. We sold tokens that were specifically to be used for PTOY blockchain network when it launched. Buyers of these tokens were basically crypto enthusiasts and early adopters of the technology who were banking on our tokens being commonplace in society. Basically, they were willing to take a risk on our project and knew that our crypto would be a digital currency of utility. Lastly, we actually had a lot of veterans purchase them because they were completely fed up with the VA and the current healthcare system.

In a way, our token sale reflected the genesis of cryptocurrency itself. The original creators of cryptocurrency were sick of the banking system's high fees and the debacle of the financial crisis in 2008. So they created a way to bank independently of current financial institutions and their rules. Veterans sought out Patientory tokens because they have been let down by our healthcare and financial system and wanted a workaround from the way healthcare is administered in America.

Part of changing the way startup financing works in America is staying flexible. Lobbying for new financing rules is certainly an alternative to be considered. But, I also think that now is the right time to regulate this new vehicle of raising capital and recognize funding with cryptocurrency, even though it's still pretty new to regulators in this country.

If you look back at history, disenfranchised people aren't alone in having to make their dreams come true creatively. Many of the great businessmen only had a dollar and a dream. But they were willing to take risks and see their dream through no matter what the setbacks. These stories inspire me especially in entrepreneurship, when you're building something from nothing. The whole message is if you can dream it, you can do it.

I'd also like to point out the benefits of not having a lot of money, because, if that's the case, there aren't many other people helping you make decisions. So when you aren't wealthy, you don't have many investors and there's more balance in the process of setting up the company. You don't want to be overfunded, but you don't want to live on the streets either.

Beyond the basics of financing, I think it's important to remember that no business is an island. The perceived value of the company revolves around its transfer of value. And that value is determined by what you as a person represent and what you are selling to the customer. To increase your financial empowerment in business, you need to surround yourself with people who can strengthen your value, which creates an environment for success. Having a customer base is the biggest validation for feeling financially empowered because, by doing so, you've discovered a solution, such as Patientory, for a big problem that's costing an industry or country, millions or even billions of dollars.

INSPIRATION

"Chrissa McFarlane made headlines for raising $7.2 million in three days via online blockchain token sales of her company Patientory. Just under 2,000 investors placed their bets on the blockchain-based distributed EMR storage computing platform."[27]

In this section, we'll focus on how to stay inspired on your roughest and toughest days. Do you know what inspires you? Have you ever really taken the time to sit down and contemplate your inspirations? Are you in need of a little inspiration today?

My inspirations have included healthcare and serving people so that they live longer, healthier lives. But I had been met by a lot of resistance. However, my team and I created 100 million tokens in order to make the dream happen. We released 70 million on the initial token sale, which netted around over $7 million. So they roughly sold at around 9 to 10 cents per token at the time. This provided the financing I needed to make Patientory happen. I had clear goals all through the process of Patientory's creation.

Why get clear on your goals and inspirations? Because they'll become your saving grace when the going gets tough and dictate your entrepreneurial path. Start the process by taking a few minutes every day for a week to only think about your inspirations. Maybe nature

---

[27] https://www.redoxengine.com/blog/bad-ass-women-in-health-tech-chrissa-mcfarlane-ceo-of-patientory/

blows you away. Maybe you get inspired by stories of survival or a really great romantic comedy. Maybe you love going to live comedy clubs or watching the ballet? Are you the dreamer who loves taking long strolls through Central Park? Or someone who likes to bring a sketchbook to a local art gallery to draw your favorite masterpiece? Do you like to take out your camera and shoot whatever you do on a Sunday afternoon and post or write about it? Do you love sports and lose yourself in catching and riding a salty sandy wave? Maybe you've got wanderlust and are plotting your next getaway.

If you're having trouble remembering what's inspiring you lately, just think back to when you were a child and remember what you really loved to do. If you have no idea what free time looks like because you've been burning the candle at both ends so long you don't even know what daylight looks like, it's time to get some balance. Pick one thing you remember you like to do and get back into it. Maybe that means playing an instrument that's been sitting in your closet forever, or just taking a five-minute walk. It doesn't have to be a big deal. Just check out things that you like to do and home in on ones that leave you feeling full of energy.

Whatever blows your hair back, find it now. Because you'll need inspirations on your worst day. Set up boundaries around your time to allow yourself the opportunity to indulge your inspirations. When you do, you'll get an energy rush from spending time doing things that inspire you. And every time you do something that inspires, it's like filling up the gas tank for handling the pressures of entrepreneurial challenges. Make sure to do those things that inspire you even when you have lots of empire-building going on. Because if you allow yourself to get depleted of inspiration by foregoing the things that inspire you, you won't last a week in the world of startup entrepreneurship.

Know that the wind is always changing so you have to stay flexible and aware. What you did last year, last month, or even yesterday might not work for your business today. In order to stay alert and agile in business, you'll need to develop the skills necessary to be a good steward of your energy.

Inspiration keeps us sharp, focused, and energized. Cooking inspires me because when I enjoy my time in the kitchen, I don't think about anything else. This breaks my pattern of obsessing over certain details and projects I have in process. This free time keeps my perspective on my business and my work-life balance in check too. And I have to say, I credit lots of Aha moments to sauces and seafood creations. I guess it has to do with my childhood memories of Mom and Dad working in the kitchen and then later when I helped at the restaurant. There's something centering about working in the kitchen. It's like my canvas where I can make as many messes as I like. After all, what are kitchens for? Breaking up our mundane routine with the activities and people we love is the ultimate tonic for inevitable energy-draining encounters in the entrepreneurial world of the Future Women.

Knowing and protecting your inspirations

Knowing and protecting your inspirations are a lot like planning for bad weather. In the entrepreneurial world of the Future Women, I'd advise that you always bring your umbrella of inspirations to protect you from the inevitable downpours.

If you need a lift today, this chapter is perfect for you. I'll be honest; discouragement is something that can really take me out sometimes. So, over time, I've learned that when I get discouraged, I go to my toolbox of self-healing that I've developed over the years. As I mentioned before, I'm a big meditator. I've really grown into it over the years and now it's just something that's a part of me. It inspires me to take time for myself to be quiet with my thoughts when I run in a world that's full of noise.

It all began around five years ago. While I did grow up in church and with religion, I wanted to connect to that same spirit I felt in church anywhere at any time. I wanted my spirituality in my life every day and found that kind of grounding through meditation. So now I have a practice that can help me center and provide a baseline of peace and tranquility in my life. Along with affirmations, this practice has had a profound influence on my life and my leadership style. More so than anything I could have bought.

I simply need to find a quiet space and close my eyes. I think the priceless peace I've gained is important to stay steady during the course of a day. I've found that I can only be an inspiration to others when I've cultivated tranquility and equanimity in my own life. This clarity and focus enables me to make the needed daily decisions to accomplish my personal and professional dreams.

Dreams are a lot like puzzles. And when we set out to solve a puzzle, the beginning is always the hardest. I remember when I was at a friend's house, she gave me a strategy to put all 5,000 pieces together. I was like *5,000 pieces? Don't you have something, you know, smaller?* But, she helped me see that if I chunked the puzzle down and made small goals, solving the puzzle was easy.

First, I needed to find the corners because they helped to define the limits and then I'd look for the straight-edged pieces to frame the puzzle. Next, I'd have to look for patterns of the puzzle's design and connect them together. Her guidance inspired me to take on the challenge of that puzzle in ways I never would have been able to before, just by helping me see an easier way to solve the problem.

I'm inspired by people who bring clarity and simplicity to struggles and obstacles I face, especially when I find myself at a crossroads. I remember after the accelerator, when I had to move back in with my parents and ended up applying to almost every graduate school because it looked like things weren't going to fly for my business. I thought, *what am I going to do now?*

Basically when I found myself at that crossroads, after some thoughtful reflection, I realized that I'd put all my self-worth on whether or not the business materialized. So my confidence and self-worth took a real beating when it didn't look like the business would happen. Even my parents were concerned about me, saying things like, "Why don't you just work for a company like everyone else?" They meant well, of course. But they didn't understand my need to launch Patientory when I had met such resistance.

What I realized about the process was that I had to be emptied of the idea of what I thought the experience would look like before I could actually invite in what was available to me. Essentially, I had to stop beating the dead horse of VC funding and get on with raising capital in new ways I couldn't yet see because I was still blinded by my expectations. But this wasn't clear to me at the time.

Honestly, I didn't recognize my life anymore once I moved in with my folks. And it all had to do with my limited expectations of the future. I had this image of who I was going to be, and all of a sudden, I was a stranger in my own life. So, I went through this intense time when I felt lost, was probably at my weakest, and almost lost hope. I became humbled in ways that got me to see things differently and opened my mind to connections I'd never have considered before. These were exactly the connections that were the missing puzzle pieces for me, you know, the ones that someone helps you find that have been lying on the floor the whole time?

FUTURE WOMAN MINDSET: Stay true to yourself.

Because of this experience, I'm really careful in my decision making and I assess things more carefully because of all that I went through. Part of what I learned is to stay true to myself. At the time I had all these different influences around me—my situation, the rejection, my inability to see how to put the pieces together, my parents who wanted my life to look a certain way. As I look back on it now, my weakest point left me the most vulnerable to influences that might have taken me off track in my life.

During these times, it's best to remind yourself of your values and your goals. Don't become what your sister wants you to be or what your significant other wants you to be either. This is an area where most people get trapped and where their dreams derail, especially when the going gets tough. Or, in my case, when the going seemed to stop completely.

I found that I really had to develop the ability to filter out the needs and wants of other people and get clear about what I valued and held dear. And most of all, when the bottom drops out, I'd recommend making sure to look for the solutions that you never considered. When I was at my lowest, I had opportunities come out of nowhere to help me along. These opportunities I recognized and harnessed because I simply had been paying attention and found myself open in new ways precisely because all the other ways I thought were possible lead me to dead ends.

FUTURE WOMAN MINDSET: Sometimes, when you're down or experiencing a lot of resistance, you close off. Do the opposite. Don't miss the rainbow after the rain.

Really, all that's truly happened in these disappointments is that your expectations hadn't been met. Once you get over the disappointment, you'll understand that your needs will be met differently than you expected. That's all. And you might take a minute or two to assess how realistic those expectations might have been.

Failure as opportunity

Silicon Valley teaches that failure is an opportunity. Some people might label what you're involved in as failure, but really, it's just an experience that leads you to another experience. There's so much judgement in the word *failure*. Take the judgement out of your experience since labels are never helpful.

And these feelings of disappointment and failure came after I'd experienced making the biggest and boldest decision I've ever made by moving out west far away from my family to attend the accelerator in Boulder. I didn't know anyone there, yet I made such amazing connections and defined my business better by discovering all these new avenues to launch Patientory that would have taken me years and years to find on my own, if ever.

But when I returned to Atlanta, I didn't immediately get any investors. My parents wondered if I had just wasted all the money I'd invested in attending the accelerator program. They had a point because I had put every last dime I'd saved and raised up until that point to attend the accelerator program. To be honest, I thought maybe they were right, and that hurt my pride big time. But it wasn't the kind of pride that got all bruised over doing something "wrong." See, I'd identified myself as an entrepreneur and now that whole identity had been called into question, simply because things didn't go the way I expected. That's not the same as being a poor entrepreneur, but I couldn't see it at the time.

I just needed to become flexible and stay tenacious. However, at that time, life found me four months further behind, nothing moving forward regarding my business, and unable to afford any additional schooling. I sort of beat myself up over the fact that if I hadn't gone to the accelerator program, I could have used the money I'd spent there to go back to school, what I felt was the only option I had left at that time. I really judged myself, and that didn't help my state of mind or my situation.

FUTURE WOMAN MINDSET: Take the judgement out of your experience since labels are never helpful.

I'd also say that even though my parents had their doubts about me and where my life was headed, they were the ones who instilled in me the idea that nothing of value comes easily. And they also taught me a lot about the kind of commitment it takes to stick with a dream, like building their restaurant. Ultimately, I took the skills they taught me and the fortitude they instilled in me to find strength in the process of defining myself in spite of the setbacks that occurred during my entrepreneurial journey.

One of the reasons I think we find it so hard to stay steady during these kinds of challenges is because it's so much harder to live with the complex "grey areas" that we face daily. It's a lot harder to live in the grey of the real world instead of the black and white of certain expectations and judgements that we make. In a way, it might be easier for minority female entrepreneurs to exercise this strength because, in my opinion, we are simply confronted by these kinds of setbacks more often than other demographics.

I come from a place where I've spent a lot of time with women trying to argue about the current state of entrepreneurship in America as being much more insidious than reality. As a result, I've come to a point where I embrace the situation and don't fight it anymore because that point of view really comes from a place of not knowing.

In reality, there's a poor track record for minority female entrepreneurs. A lot of financial investors want to give money in a scientific way so that their investment hedges on past performance. Well, when you don't have anything (not even an industry, in my case) to compare it to, they decide to not open their wallets. I understand that, but instead of arguing about the current state of affairs, we need to change that narrative. In order to change that narrative, everyone has to be aware of the current narrative and of their work, what they're worth and how they're treated and accepted in the collective work environment.

FUTURE WOMAN MINDSET: Instead of arguing about the current state of affairs we need to change the narrative.

In other words, we'll no longer be conforming to a thought that there are no successful minority female entrepreneurs. **Instead, we'll be creating a narrative about why you, as a minority female entrepreneur, are worthy of the investment based on your applicable experiences, past quantifiable results, and related educational and career trajectories.**

Why aren't there more minority entrepreneurs?

In a way, I believe the subject of this book is a metaphor for Patientory.

Female minority entrepreneurship in America is similar to the interest I'm trying to create in the new industry we're birthing at Patientory. Both *Future Women* and Patientory are formations of big movements in the world that need to exist and be nurtured in order to help the world leverage the strengths of the marginalized and vulnerable: minority female entrepreneurs and healthcare patients, respectively.

I'd like to explore some of the answers to why there aren't more minority entrepreneurs. It's imperative that we become leaders in the new economy, but beyond that, we also need to be a socially interactive group so that we can live and inspire others. At this time, we have the networking capability unlike any we've seen before. It's about reframing the narratives that are being put upon us by misinformed people. It's about taking charge by assuming our places at the table and having our voices heard so we can define and be a part of the new narrative. It's important that people get out and tell their story and say what's going on in a real way—one that's productive, enlightening, and uplifting. Ultimately, it's important for us to have transparency, equal access, and trust.

Blockchain transforms power from the "powers that be" into the hands of private citizens the same way that Patientory is transforming the access and management of healthcare data from big companies to individuals and in the same way I know female minority entrepreneurs will transform the world of entrepreneurship.

My transformation from "hacker house" dweller to entrepreneur happened in a way I never expected. At the accelerator program in Boulder, we had a series of mentors whom we worked with each week, from product to market, and tech to finance. You name it, we had mentors for everything! In one of those meetings, I met with a tech agent who informed me about blockchain. I had heard about blockchain before because of Bitcoin, but I didn't really understand how it would apply to the type of business I was interested in building. So I went on a deep dive of digging into research and development and really getting into our business proposal with the intention of figuring out our business value in relation to using blockchain technology.

I don't even think my mentors made the connection in terms of how blockchain would affect my business model and actually fit at Patientory. They had just mentioned blockchain as a new technology that people looked at from a security perspective. When I began to apply it to my business model and they actually helped me understand how it could help with integration of data, then I decided to dig even deeper. It seemed like a part of the puzzle was missing, the integral piece regarding the architecture I had built out and how it would really fit in with the industry in terms of interoperability.

The added security blockchain provided presented a new business model that we hadn't considered before. I did more research on blockchain, the light bulb just went off in my head, and I thought, *this makes sense.* It solved the interoperability problem that the healthcare industry had been trying to tackle for over twenty years. The accelerator in Colorado really helped me begin to connect all the dots and know the true value of what blockchain would mean to my company.

So, long story short, I went to Boulder to get the answers to my business struggles and found the answer by putting all the pieces together at home in my own backyard. But, I never would have been attuned to blockchain if I hadn't been introduced to it at the accelerator program in that mentor meeting.

Say blockchain to most people, and you'll light up the eyes of a small percentage of people, but my mom was pretty mystified by it. Sonia's

Bootcamp never had a class on blockchain; let's just put it that way. So, my mom was amazed every day at the developments that led to Patientory. One time, she told me, "That's why God gave you this vision and not me because no one can see your vision but you." And she went on to say that she would have given up on the same mission a long time ago. It was wonderful to experience her pride when everything came together for Patientory, especially since she and Dad thought I had given up on my dreams along the way.

And when you're lying on your mom and dad's sofa, listening to their old vinyl music records and staring at the ceiling tiles because you've felt you've lost your direction, you'll find that developing and sticking to your own vision is your only ticket out. **Since you can foster any vision in the world, be sure it's important,** important enough that it will involve a struggle. And when you're finally vulnerable enough to realize that you have a lot to learn, begin to check out and stay curious about all the ways your vision can succeed that you hadn't expected or even dared to dream of.

If you're reading this and you're on the sofa, know that it's just a season. And if you haven't bottomed out yet, it's a statistical certainty that you will in some form or another in the future. If you're there, try embracing it because actually hitting bottom is a gift. You'll see things in new ways and become conscious of opportunities you never would have if you hadn't bottomed-out. And the only way up is to follow the breadcrumbs of your own experience and no one else's.

Vibrating high, even as you're scrambling to find a way to have a business meeting while your mom is vacuuming, is crucial. I learned this in elementary school when I had my first big transformational experience. I went from being a "C" student, to a Salutatorian. Along the way, during my education, I kept hearing things like, *if you can dream it, you can achieve it.* I heard these same kinds of high-vibration sayings off and on growing up. With the help of my community and my parents, I was able to appreciate small wins and small transformations like getting over being the girl who couldn't get "A's" because those girls over there got them.

FUTURE WOMAN MINDSET: Don't take anything personally.

Who and what inspires me

As I got my start in telemedicine, I kept up with the latest and greatest female entrepreneurs in healthcare. It's staggering to become familiar with the statistics. Women make up half of the world's population but the primary healthcare decisions are made 90% of the time by women for their families. Putting that into numbers, close to 4 billion women need access to accurate and efficient healthcare not only for themselves but also for those they love and care for.

These women, women like you, inspire me every day. While 50% of the global workforce consists of women [28] , we are woefully underrepresented in the tech world where our insights and experience could be best put to use. We are the authority on healthcare in America because we're the ones who are on the battlefield every day, fighting for excellent healthcare for ourselves and our families.

If men are the ones making all the decisions while women are being left out of tech, people who don't make healthcare calls as much as women will develop systems that are blind to not only our experience and wealth of knowledge but also our particular healthcare needs. And

---

[28] https://ourworldindata.org/female-labor-force-participation-key-facts

those blind spots can prove deadly.

America is dead last for maternal mortality in the industrial world.[29] And that appalling statistic alone needs to be changed and changed fast. I'm inspired by challenges like these and find inspiration from the entrepreneurs with boots on the ground in the battle to turn the tide for women in healthcare.

Kate Ryder, CEO of Maven Clinic Co., a telemedicine services company for women is one of my inspirations. Maven Clinic provides many services that have been long forgotten in our modern healthcare system including on-demand access to fertility experts, pregnancy and postpartum specialists, and back-to-work coaches who help new mothers and families juggle a career and family needs. She even used Maven to guide her through her pregnancies and help her transition back to work as CEO. Her series B funding led the company to raise $27 million.

> *"When I started Maven in 2014, the inspiration was all around me: I was working in venture capital in London covering the emerging digital health sector. It was around the same time that my friends started having kids and I noticed the gaps in care that exist at every life stage, but appear to get bigger when women start a family."*
> —Kate Ryder, CEO Maven Clinic Co.

FUTURE WOMAN MINDSET: Fill the gaps with entrepreneurial companies.

I'm an avid reader and listener of podcasts. An endless list of spiritual and inspirational titles kept me focused on how to build Patientory the

---

[29] https://www.npr.org/2017/05/12/528098789/u-s-has-the-worst-rate-of-maternal-deaths-in-the-developed-world

right way. I have some of my go-to resources listed at the end of the book too, in case you want to check them out. You can take a peek at them when you need an extra dose of encouragement.

Some of the resources find me in funny ways. I like to say that it's a good idea to put yourself in as many networking experiences as possible because a lot of the time, the resources you need will find you in that way. For example, I'm a part of HIMSS, Health Information Management Systems Society, a nonprofit membership organization based on the U.S. and one of the largest healthcare nonprofits. They do so much education and continuing education about healthcare technology. I'm actually on their Interoperability Committee, which requires committee members to attend mandatory kick-off meetings. At one of these meetings, a book was laid out on a table when my fellow members and I walked into the conference room. One of my colleagues asked if the book was for us. It wasn't but the staff suggested that we each take one anyway. So I happened to open a book called *Engage! Transforming Healthcare Through Digital Patient Engagement* and I've found it to be an interesting bit of information that I never would have sought out on my own.

Currently, I'm listening to *Bad Blood: Secrets and Lies in a Silicon Valley Startup* by John Carreyrou, about a healthcare tech entrepreneur Elizabeth Holmes, former Founder of failed Theranos, a company that had been valued at about 10 billion dollars which dropped to zero overnight. The media had called her the female Steve Jobs because she carefully crafted her message wearing almost entirely black outfits and turtleneck sweaters, like Jobs did.

She will go on trial for fraud soon and is being accused, along with her former President and CEO Ramesh "Sunny" Balwani, of deliberately misleading investors, policymakers, and the public about the accuracy of Theranos's blood-testing technologies. Here's a quote from Holmes during a *Vanity Fair* event when she was at the top of her game:

> *"What I want to say, especially to the young women in the room here, do everything you can to be the best in science and math and engineering. It's our actions that will determine this new stereotype around women being the best and how we will become the best at science, math and engineering and it's that that our little girls will see when they determine who they want to be when they grow up."*
> — Elizabeth Holmes

I guess the question becomes, *can we be inspired by spectacular dishonesty and failure?* I'm not sure if you can call her story inspiring. Rather, it's more a call to action, which is a form of inspiration, I guess. Her sentiment is a wonderful message for today's young Future Women; however, unfortunately for us, Holmes didn't realize that her actions affect us all. It's important to be aware of the cautionary, success-at-all-costs tales. It's definitely important to note that greed has been and will always be an ill of the entrepreneurial experience. That's why it's important to have great boards in place and great transparency with investors.

FUTURE WOMAN MINDSET: Don't let cautionary tales frame the narrative.

Holmes dropped out of Stanford at nineteen to found a healthcare diagnostic company where a prick of blood from your finger would diagnose whatever risks you had for disease without using a needle. She sold the allegedly fictitious technology to Walmart, Walgreens, and had multimillion-dollar contracts that raised over $800 million from investors. Then the business she built over the course of fifteen years tumbled down because of a whistleblower, an intern who reported that the company testing had been a fraud. Apparently, all of their demos were fabricated.

It's a cautionary tale to inspire you to follow your values and never let business get in the way of good science and common sense. She had values, just the wrong kind. So cling tight to your network and help each other learn and lead with cautionary tales of the past while dreaming boldly about the future. To that end, enjoy joining as many committees as you have time for and keep learning from others to keep you inspired to go your own way.

Another book that has helped to shape my entrepreneurial journey is *The Alchemist*, by Paulo Coelho, a beautifully written book that describes the journey of being in touch with who you are and knowing your passions. One of my passions includes spending time with my family because they inspire and rejuvenate me like nothing else. Belly laughing and going to family events grounds me in ways that feed my soul. I also love traveling, and it's a good thing, too, because I travel a lot on behalf of the company. Whenever I travel for work, I study a bit about the place I'm visiting and learn about the city by going on a walking tour whenever possible. I love learning about different cultures and how we're all tied together.

FUTURE WOMAN MINDSET: Dream boldly about the future.

Taking a walk with the pioneers

Whenever I think I have it tough, it always helps me to consider the paths that minority female entrepreneurs have taken. I hope you find inspiration from their varied and full stories and a nugget or two for your Future Woman walk.

I remember how much I loved Black History month during my elementary and middle school years. It was like the month of February gave me permission to dig a little deeper and learn more about the females who shaped their own future.

I remember first learning and reading about Ida B. Wells, and Sojourner Truth. My reports on both women made it to the school's showcase and the principle posted my work up near her office. Every time I walked by the auditorium, I stepped a little more confidently at the sight of my research on the wall of women, celebrated only one month out of the year.

Ida B. Wells

Freedom meant a whole new world to freed slaves but something entirely different to White Segregationists after the Civil War. After the 13th and 14th Amendment were signed into law, things didn't really go the way the freed slaves had anticipated. The people threatened by the freedom of the slaves, those holding all the cards in the power structure before the Emancipation Proclamation, worked hard to take those freedoms away.

Growing up in Memphis, Ida B. Wells got her start as a teacher but then turned her talents to investigative journalism. Co-owner of a newspaper called *Free Speech and Headlight* located in downtown Memphis, she gained a reputation as a courageous, fiercely independent champion of the truth in her reporting as well as an ardent feminist before anyone even heard of the word.

When her friend Thomas Moss was murdered by a mob, it changed her life forever. Thomas was a Black entrepreneur who was part-owner of the People's Grocery, a food co-op, located in South Memphis known as "the curve," a place where Black entrepreneurs could thrive. It was a place of community where Black people could purchase their goods from Black business owners.

White men felt the People's Grocery took away from their profits, and after an altercation between young Black boys and White boys outside of the grocery turned violent, the men who owned the cooperative defended their property. They were arrested and thrown in jail. When seventy-five White men came to the jail in the middle of the night, they took three men, including Thomas, all upstanding men in the community, sent them on a rail car a little way out of town, then shot them to death. Thomas was a sterling citizen with a young daughter, and at the time of his murder, his wife was pregnant. Ms. Wells was their daughter's godmother.

Ida got a tip that the mob had headed to the jail and reported on it. Up until this time, Memphis was seen as a relatively safe place from lynching. But this incident changed everything. Lynching instilled terror in the Black population and had been used to keep Black people down economically. Emboldened by the injustice of her friend's death, Ida used her paper to expose White people behind the lynching. As a result, White people destroyed her offices while she happened to be out of town. When Ida received lynching threats if she ever returned, she chose to never live in Memphis again but kept up her advocacy.

FUTURE WOMAN MINDSET: Be a courageous, fiercely independent champion of the truth. (Sojourner Truth)

"Truth is powerful and it prevails."

—Sojourner Truth

Born Isabelle Bumfrey, a slave in New York in 1797, she only spoke Dutch. At the age of nine, she was sold together with a flock of sheep for $100. She had suffered many hardships, including bearing five children with an older slave who her third master made her marry.

She eventually escaped to Canada and returned to the U.S. to New York City to work as a housekeeper for a Christian evangelist, Ellijah Pierson, after becoming a devout Christian. She began to help Ellijah Pierson with street-corner preaching. In 1843 she heard a voice from heaven and this began her mission of spreading "God's truth and plan for salvation."

Soon after, at the age of 46, she gave herself a new name, Sojourner Truth, and became a "traveling preacher," what she considered to be the meaning of her new name. She would later say that, "the spirit calls me and I must go." She made her way in the world, traveling and preaching The Good News, talking about the abolition of slavery, and even met with President Abraham Lincoln during the Civil War. She became a popular speaker in the Abolitionist movement of the time and spoke about women's rights as well.

FUTURE WOMAN MINDSET: Go where the spirit leads. (Rihanna)

"Everyone knows Rihanna as a wonderful singer, but through our partnership at Fenty Beauty, I have discovered a true entrepreneur, a true CEO and a great leader."
> —Bernard Arnault, President and CEO of LVMH

As Mr. Arnault said, everyone knows Rihanna as a pop star, but in 2017, she actually made a conscious decision to not make any more music. Instead, she invested her time, talents, and resources into opening her own fashion business. She started out with makeup, then over the past two-and-a-half years, she's evolved that into fashion. The year she opened, she got acquired by LVMH, which is the largest luxury fashion house for luxury goods and cosmetics. Her brand, Fenty, is the first Black-woman-owned luxury company to be acquired by the luxury brand LVMH, based in Paris. Rhianna is also the first Black woman to have a luxury company valued at over a hundred million dollars.

She took the opportunity as a singer to fuel her entrepreneurship. Even though her fans are constantly asking when she will make more music, she's still held to her values and beliefs and is happy to find what she really wants to do for her professional life. She didn't let anyone change her mind, and I find that inspiring.

FUTURE WOMAN MINDSET: Hold to your values and beliefs. (Serena Williams)

"The success of every woman should be the inspiration to another. We should raise each other up. Make sure you're very courageous: be strong, be extremely kind, and above all be humble."

—Serena Williams

Serena's husband is both a technology entrepreneur and venture capitalist and perhaps this influence continues to help stake her claim in the world of technology. Because of her status, intelligence, and influence, she was able to build the ability to also invest capital in minority female businesses like Mahmee. She also has a foot in the world of healthcare because of her recent journey into motherhood and all of the health issues she has faced in her career as a world-champion professional athlete.

FUTURE WOMAN MINDSET: Build on your intelligence and influence to lift up other female entrepreneurs. (Angela Davis)

"I will no longer accept the things I cannot change; I will change the things I cannot accept."

—Angela Davis

I remember sitting in my Africana Studies class at Cornell University taught by Professor Turner, Dean Janice Turner's husband who was an integral part in starting the first Africana Studies major at an Ivy League institution. One day, Angela Davis walked in to teach our class.

A master scholar who studied at the Sorbonne, Davis is an activist, scholar, and writer who advocates for the oppressed. At one time, she had been thrown in jail for murder charges accused of aiding in a prison outbreak, but she was ultimately cleared. A member of the communist party until the early 1990s, her passions include advocating for gender equity, prison reform, and alliances across color lines. She grew up in a middle-class neighborhood in Birmingham, AL, dubbed "Dynamite Hill" because of all the African-American homes there that had been bombed by the Ku Klux Klan. She'd also known some of the four African-American girls killed in the 1963 Birmingham church bombing. She eventually spent her life teaching at UCLA and The University of California Santa Cruz.

I sat in the first row, as usual, and was struck by Angela Davis's story and experiences. The shyness that I never quite grew out of even in college had been surpassed only by the admiration I had for her even though I barely knew her story before enrolling in the class. I couldn't find the courage in my bones to even raise my hand and ask her a question that day.

That was an important day in solidifying my decision to pursue Africana studies as opposed to the Biology major my peers in pre-med declared. I never looked back and don't regret that decision.

"I like to think that historical memory is important. 1968 was probably the year more happened in my political life than other years. Dr. Martin Luther King was assassinated. I had been a member of the Black Panther Party and then joined the Snick Party and then also joined the communist party," she said. I was all ears.

If it weren't for Professor Turner's wife, Dean Janice Turner, the Dean of the College of Arts and Sciences, I would have never taken the class or had the opportunity to meet Angela Davis. But I grumbled that August prior to enrolling in the class when Dean Janice Turner recommended that I take the class taught by her husband, thinking in the back of my head this wasn't going to make it as a requirement for me as a Biology major. Besides, I could always watch documentaries about Black History in America, but I decided to give it a try.

If it weren't for Dean Janice Turner taking a chance on me, I wouldn't have pursued my current journey. I'll never forget the day I sat across from her in the office at the campus of Weill Cornell Medical College that rainy spring afternoon. I was a senior in high school and she looked at me and said, "Chrissa, your SATs aren't as competitive as your peers. You have excellent grades and laboratory research experience and medical experience, more than the average high school student, but why do you want to attend Cornell? Why do you want to be a doctor?"

Why did I want to be a doctor?

I thought about everything the Dean had said. My passion for healthcare began as a dream when I was a little girl and continued throughout high school, when I conducted microbiology research at the Albert Einstein College of Medicine and won top honors in the city of New York. Fortunately, she had been impressed by that. But, I didn't really have a great answer to her question. I knew why I wanted to be in healthcare—I wanted to serve others in the healthcare field. But I didn't know the how; did I really want to be a doctor? Later on, I decided that I really didn't and there was another path that I would follow on my road to service in healthcare. I knew that if I followed my heart, the way to serve in the healthcare field would reveal itself to me at the appropriate time.

There were only three months left of high school when I spoke with Dean Janice Turner, and I had automatically been accepted to Stony Brook University, along with everyone else who was in the top 10% of the graduating class at Bronx Science. At that time, I'd been waitlisted at Harvard and ached to get into at least one of my reach schools. Luckily, Dean Turner gave me a chance. Little did I know getting into Cornell would expose me to a diverse and rich history only taught at that school at that time.

FUTURE WOMAN MINDSET: Know your why.

TRANSFORMATION

"Atlanta is a fantastic environment to start and grow a company. Whether it's making introductions, or serving as a mentor, there is a refreshing attitude of—how can I help? There's also a strong diversity initiative that doesn't seem to exist in quite the same way in other cities."

—Chrissa McFarlane

I never dreamt of being the first woman CEO of a blockchain company that's poised to revolutionize the healthcare industry. The transformation I've experienced from seeing myself as one of the "lesser than" girls in school—someone who wasn't ever going to be part of the "other girls" who received A's on their schoolwork and were also popular among the boys—to founding my own company hasn't happened easily or overnight. As I leave my twenties, I realize I have much more to learn. I look forward to the unfolding wisdom that the next decade of my life will bring. In crossing this threshold I have a major goal in mind—creating more Future Women.

So how do we go about becoming Future Women today?

What does it look like to lift each other up?

As we decide to take our entrepreneurial experience to the next level, we can take a realistic look at how to define the new narrative by becoming aware of the issues being faced by us but not being talked about today. And studying these issues in greater context so that they may be adequately understood by current and next generations of Future Women.

I feel the need to deeply change not only the narrative, but also the demographics of female minority entrepreneurship. As a Black woman founder in the worlds of tech, blockchain, cryptocurrency, and healthcare, you can bet I didn't see anyone who looked like me sitting around the table. Thankfully, companies are trying to change that narrative so that the captains at the helm of the industries of the future will be more inclusive.

Our transformation is long in coming. If you look at the history of female empowerment, the process has taken us through women's suffrage to civil rights, to becoming elected officials where the dream of a female president is within reach as more female candidates run for the presidency.

But around the world, we have a long way to go. Saudi Arabia only recently passed a law allowing a woman to drive. Honestly, it's hard to stomach the absurdity about the way women are treated around the world. Many women are so busy fetching water for their families that they can't even dream of pursuing their education. The statistics are very overwhelming when we consider how women meet amazing challenges all over the world.

However, you don't have to look far to find tough statistics for women in America, particularly the highest mortality rate for mothers in the industrialized Western world. So we have a lot of work to do to lift each other up. In order to become the Future Women the world needs, we have to be able to take our negative experiences and turn them into opportunities. Persistence, grit, and resilience will be the keys.

A timeline of female empowerment

"One can perfectly well philosophize while cooking supper."
—Sor Juana Inés de la Cruz of Mexico, celebrated writer,
memorably defended women's rights to gain an education
in 1691. She appears on Mexican currency today.

Since I love to cook, I couldn't agree more, of course. For me, in the field of healthcare, female empowerment all started with Agnodice in 400 BC. Recognized as one of the first female gynecologists, she courageously practiced medicine in Greece when women could be killed for using their healing skills. When she was caught by the authorities and almost sent to her death for practicing medicine, patients who came to her defense rescued her and she was allowed to continue to practice medicine as a result.

Her patients rescued her. I think we can learn from her ancient story of redemption as we find echoes of Future Women coming to each other's rescue in our day and age.

Fast forward to 1893 when Kate Sheppard boldly presented a petition to New Zealand's Parliament demanding women's suffrage with a whopping total of 32,000 signatures, a "signature" move that put New Zealand in the history books as the first self-governing country to grant national voting rights to women that year. Just fifty years later, women would be the backbone of the workforce in the U.S.

"Over six million women joined the workforce by the end of WWII, and by 1945, they made up almost 37% of the workforce, up from only 27% in 1940. Their contributions were crucial to the war effort. In the aircraft industry alone, women made up 65% of all employees."

During the war, women worked all kinds of jobs from pounding out torpedoes in munition factories to shipbuilding in boatyards. They built airplanes, drove fire trucks, fought fires, were conductors of trains and trams, and healed the sick, mostly as nurses.

Dr. Margaret Craighill was the first woman physician to become a commissioned officer in the U.S. Army in 1943. The signing of the Sparkman-Johnson Bill into law by President Franklin Roosevelt gave her the opportunity to do so because it was the first time women were allowed to enter the Army and Navy Medical Corps. Before President Roosevelt's ink was dry, Dr. Margaret D. Craighill, Dean of the Women's Medical College of Pennsylvania at the time, requested a leave of absence from her job and joined the armed forces one month later.

While women saved the day during the war, afterwards, things went back to the way they were almost overnight. The freedom and confidence women gained by earning a paycheck and doing valuable work evaporated quickly because the returning soldiers needed work in order to lay claim to their old civilian lives. So the very people who had once begged and recruited women to meet their workloads now sent them back to the kitchen so that their jobs could be given to the returning soldiers. Kind of hard to serve spaghetti after you've built an airplane.

As a result, women working in the U.S. workforce fell to 32.7%, according to the U.S. Department of Labor, despite the fact that an earlier poll showed that between 60% to 70% of women wanted to remain in their jobs in peacetime.

But you can't unring the bell. Women had begun to work and work well. They set their sights on advocating for their working rights, including equality of pay and opportunity in the workplace. In the last seventy years, revolutionary changes occurred with women at work. From the end of WWII in 1945 to 1995, women entered the workplace in staggering numbers.

And as they did, their ranks rose and they soon began to assume managerial positions in corporate America with global reach. In the 1970s, a turning point occurred when female entrepreneurship became a reality as a result of the feminist movement, which instigated national legislation for equal opportunity in the workplace. The late 1980s found women owning half of all American businesses and they would also soon become 30% of all MBA degree holders. By the turn of the millennium, three American women headed companies with earnings over a billion U.S. dollars.

Superstar entrepreneurs from Martha Stewart to Oprah Winfrey and Carole Black have helped to wage successful battles against the glass ceiling and other barriers to female entrepreneurship because they pushed back on the ideology of traditional woman's role, an ideology of domesticity that still influences the way female entrepreneurship is perceived today.

When things don't work out (then end up working out for the best)

My dream was to be a surgeon, but that didn't work out. So I had to take a new path and transform my dream into something else. Something that ended up being more uniquely me than the path I'd originally chosen.

Back in elementary school, like everyone I suppose, I struggled with taking exams. I was in public school and labeled a "gifted student" or in "honors" programs, and all that involved a great deal of test taking. The programs I qualified for always required doing well on exams, whether gaining access to an honors class or a private school.

I remember preparing for two summers, two days a week after school, and on Saturdays for two years straight in order to take a specialized high school test to get into one of New York City's prestigious standardized high schools. The school I got accepted to boasted more Nobel Prize Winners than any country in the world. The summers felt heavy and grueling instead of carefree. Through this experience of driving hard to achieve my dreams, a part of me burnt out. I learned through this process that there's great power in rest and restoration.

I think the experiences of having to achieve on tests and constantly driving myself to improve my scores grew a lot of anxiety within me around test taking. When I got to Cornell, I, like everyone else, had to take what they call "weed-out classes," and, that year, I ended up with a "C" in General Chemistry. This was my first C, the rest of my grades had all been As and Bs. So my GPA was affected and then my MCATs weren't as competitive, so I faced a lot of rejection when I applied to medical school.

I ended up getting into a Caribbean medical school, but my pride got in the way of going there because I felt that if I had attended Cornell, I should be able to do better. But, in order to get my GPA up to become more competitive, especially coming from Cornell, I would have to invest in more schooling and many more hours of homework and test taking.

At that point, I definitely had to do some introspection and ask myself some life-defining questions, which led me to a big decision. Of the many questions I had, one stood out. I asked myself, *Is investing in more schooling really something that I'm called to do?* Even though I'd heard of people who had gone the extra schooling route and brought up their GPA, that road wasn't the road for me. Because I closed the door on the opportunity to go to medical school, another opened that landed me in the business of healthcare.

FUTURE WOMAN MINDSET: Opportunity lies just past those "closed doors."

All the while that I was at Cornell I had been transforming in small and big ways. I explored a liberal arts education, which taught me how to think analytically and solve problems innovatively because I had studied how people throughout history had done the same. I became exposed to a part of myself I had only begun to understand with exposure to Africana studies, a new major at the time, and exposure to Angela Davis and many other global thought leaders and movers and shakers of our time.

In my junior year at Cornell, they had started offering an entrepreneurship class in biomedical sciences. The first-time offering intrigued me, so I enrolled in the class. The Liberal Arts college also had joint courses with the Business college, which gave me the opportunity to learn from professors who talked about entrepreneurship and sciences. This curriculum had never been offered in the liberal arts coursework before and would become even more transformative in my professional life. For me, the timing of the entrepreneurial class and access to the business college gave me a unique exposure to the worlds of business and medicine. I became open to different aspects of life and saw different perspectives than I had before.

There wasn't any monumental moment that occurred in my

entrepreneurial business class experience that flicked a switch in me to create Patientory. But the constant exposure to the idea of seeing how different researchers and scientists applied their discoveries and the products that they invented intrigued me and gave me the idea that simple solutions can improve the lives of millions of people. They didn't practice medicine but, rather, transformed the medical arts because of their discoveries.

I realized that my sphere of influence in the right discovery would be so much larger than that of a doctor in private practice. In the best of practices the most people that you can directly help would be in the hundreds or, if you're really dedicated, in the thousands. My liberal arts discipline helped me develop a philosophy and a theory that what I would learn in the sciences were things that I'd rarely use daily. But, if I went into a graduate program for business, I might have the ability to discover a way to help more people with a technology that would be used every day, helping a vast number of people.

I developed connections that inspired me during my entrepreneurial class at Cornell and decided to go to business school through a small new program they had for liberal arts graduates. There were about sixty of us and the program catered to liberal arts graduates who were one or two years out of college without a business background. This exposed me to more business acumen, and I got to hear from people like Steve Reinemund, the Dean of the Business college and the former CEO of PepsiCo.

In addition to hosting us at his house for breakfast, (which I always thought was crazy because that meant he had around fifty business students in his home early in the morning) he brought in Ursula Burns, the Black female CEO of Xerox, who spoke to our class. She inspired me because in meeting her, I experienced someone who looked like me and held a CEO leadership position of a Fortune 500 company. If she could do it, I felt that I could do it too. Being exposed to other female leaders in business really painted that picture of possibility for me in the business world.

Steve Reinemund's legacy is an example for younger entrepreneurs and future business leaders to help foster the attitude of following your passions in business. I would say his favorite word was integrity. Overall, the experience of having him as my Dean and attending his lectures was transformational because the work we accomplished quickly took me from my traditional service mindset in healthcare to all the possibilities that awaited me in tying that healthcare-service concept to the business world. Because of that switch in my mindset, I consulted for a pharmacy and received much more hands-on work. This pharmacy experience would lead me to create the idea of Patientory because I began to understand what was lacking in our current healthcare infrastructure.

The information I received in these classes and experiences still stay with me. Just the other day, while traveling to meet a new business partner, I saw a quote from Angela Davis painted on the side of a building as I walked back to my hotel. It's the quote about no longer accepting the things she cannot change. And it was like a wink from my past to stay strong in the here-and-now and on into the future. Her words have always been a touchstone for me. And her words there on that otherwise plain brick building reminded me to stay committed to raising up minority female entrepreneurs.

Women at Patientory

"We must also lift as we climb."

—Angela Davis

GSU Clinical Informatics Interns

As I write this book, I currently have six minority women summer interns working at Patientory. These women from the Georgia State University (GSU) Byrdine F. Lewis College of Nursing and Health Professions were inspired to work with me because they wanted to get firsthand experience from a woman who is currently building a company in healthcare. They were chosen to intern with Patientory for the Summer Clinical Health Informatics two-month program.

The students are studying the field of health informatics, which is the design and implementation of IT-related information in healthcare. It can be considered a cross between healthcare, information science, and computer science. Those innovations can cover security and electronic delivery and management of medical records. It's a fairly new field of study, as only in 2009 were medical records first required to be maintained in an electronic form. The GSU Lewis College of Nursing and Health Professions took its first health informatics students in 2013 and launched a graduate program in 2016. Both programs are unique because they're the only interdisciplinary program in the United States in the field of health informatics.

With the staff of Patientory as their guides, they're working alongside the developers of blockchain technology as applied to healthcare. The Patientory system will educate them about various forms of cryptocurrency, a universally-centered patient database, and a way to securely share information from it. All of those are used in combination to increase security and make healthcare results more accurate and available. The blockchain system ensures that records cannot be changed without a trail and that any access can be controlled by those with the key.

The Atlanta Tech Village, where Patientory has its office, is the startup gathering place for Atlanta's many technological businesses. Members are supported in a variety of tasks in the community with the goal of connecting those with ideas, those with talent to the capital they need. It is one of the top five tech centers in the whole United States. Marketing and business development teams from the Tech Village assist the interns in their work and analysis.

Both of those factors will combine to give the interns a first-class look in how to apply everything they've learned in the classroom to a real-life setting. The intersection of healthcare and computer management that Patientory puts to use every day is a prime example of how health informatics works in the real world.

Every Friday during the internship period, they will be able to attend a conference detailing some basic ways to get a job in the industry and other ways of learning and dealing with the many problems that might come up in their future careers—from dealing with diversity in the workplace to managing stress on the job. Speakers will include the co-founder of the Atlanta Tech Village as well as founders of two different startups.

With the number of startups at the Tech Village at this point, any intern there would have a good chance of finding their future employer. They came in prepared to work and they've hit the ground running from the moment they arrived. They were very positive, team-oriented, and worked hard as a team to do great work together.

Overcoming the blind spots

Blind spot: *n.* An area in which one fails to exercise judgment or discrimination.

Growing a business, especially as a female isn't an easy feat. Blind spots come in many different forms. The most prevalent blind spot I've encountered, and the most common in any startup, in my opinion, is finding the right people. The process can be both a positive and a negative. Throughout the life cycle of my business, I've come across people who are like wolves in sheep's clothing. They represent one thing and are very cunning then turn out to be someone else after we begin a working relationship.

I think the hardest challenge for me as an entrepreneur is finding the right people. I really had to grow thick skin in order to know when people weren't the right fit. This eye-opening process of transformation and building a business has found me comfortable with the notion that some people will be with my company for a season, and some people are on a much longer journey. On the flip side are those who are beautiful souls but just not skilled enough to move to the next level. If these people aren't extracted from the business at the appropriate time, they can become dead weight and end up doing more harm than good.

FUTURE WOMAN MINDSET: Be comfortable with the uncomfortable and challenge yourself to go outside your comfort zone.

Running a startup company is all about the search and discovery of quality, talented people and surrounding yourself with people who can help you achieve success and the goals you set out for your company. A wise person once said, "A team is not a group of people who work together. A team is a group of people who trust each other." I couldn't agree more. Future Women have to learn how to set the bar high when choosing the right people for the business.

Besides picking the right people, another blind spot involves situations in which people accept intolerable treatment just because they've gotten used to unhealthy patterns. I mentioned that I began my journey to go into business for myself because of the toxic culture I experienced at my first startup. I had let my situation get so bad that it became hard to accomplish my work daily. I found myself going home with nose bleeds and mental exhaustion to the point that I didn't even find the time to eat. I'd just fall asleep after shutting the door behind me after my commute from work. I had to set boundaries around the kind of treatment I would and wouldn't tolerate. I had to become aware of those boundaries first and then act when they were violated.

Taking the journey to find yourself isn't an easy feat, but part of our transformation into Future Women occurs when we get a clear vision of our values and what we stand for. So many catalysts can become our defining moments. If we've been pushed into a transition because of life-changing or traumatic experiences, we can always use them to learn about ourselves in ways that will continue to guide us to become the people we're meant to be. These are truly life's valuable lessons that serve as a kind of compass to alert you that you're headed off course and may need to steer to the left or right in order to stay on your path to overall success.

Sharing your journey with others

I believe strongly in being of service to others. In my goal of transforming the lives of women through minority entrepreneurial success, I served as co-chair of the healthcare industry's HIMSS18 Blockchain Workgroup, serve on HIMSS Interoperability & Health Information Exchange Committee, and speak at industry conferences globally to educate people about new technologies and to inspire other businesswomen and entrepreneurs. To advance education about blockchain and cryptocurrency, I participate in coauthoring journal articles, being interviewed in national and industry press, and make occasional appearances on Bloomberg Live. Last year, I was asked to cut the ribbon to open the 2018 Arab Health Conference in Dubai, a city which has now set its sights on becoming the world's first blockchain city by 2020.

While I've been participating in a small-group leader training at church, it resonated with me that there was another way for me to help empower other women in my generation. As a woman, navigating your career isn't always easy. Support is key to success; so, I started a Future Women group at church to share my story and help other women enter the world of entrepreneurism. I found meeting with like-minded women in this group gave them perspective and real-world information that would help them shape their careers in ways they never thought about before.

FUTURE WOMAN MINDSET: Share your perspectives and help give real-world information to other women in order to help shape their careers.

And you never know when that kind of opportunity will present itself. For instance, I participated as a mentor in an incubator called Digital Undivided, which is a space where Black and Lantinx women founders come together with their big ideas and high growth companies to receive training, network and gain access to the funding that can create startups that the world had never seen before. Their motto is "Go big, or go home."

I learned so much about what entrepreneurial success can look like from the Black and Latinx perspective by meeting and learning from other founders who looked just like me. The organization has a passion for taking the unmatched grit and hustle of minority entrepreneurs and bringing them out of the shadows to not only get noticed, but also get into the spotlight to make their groundbreaking, game-changing dreams come true with connections to funding that wouldn't occur in today's VC climate. They basically invest where traditional VCs won't. By going big without asking permission, they have helped build 52 companies, raise $25 million in investments, and reached 2,000 founders.

So when I arrived, I was ready to soak up all the connections I could and never imagined that my story would inspire someone. But it did. I met Farrah Allen, CEO of The Labz, whom I wrote about earlier in the Minority & Mindset chapter, during my mentorship session at Digital Undivided. I had met her at other events around the city but never got to learn what her company did. After hearing my VC investment story, she decided to incorporate blockchain into her technology offering, an online platform where account holders can collaborate on musical projects through the security of blockchain, which, in turn, clarifies ownership and royalty percentage splits.

"All these people and all these assets are just rolling around," founder and CEO, Farah Allen said to Hypepotamus. "All these things aren't tied to people's identities. They're not copyrighted, and people don't get paid."

The platform, described as the Google Drive for music, allows artists to upload and create tracks with other artists directly through an online portal that verifies the percentage of contribution of each creator.

"The process of collaborating was a lot of the process that I was solving in the corporate world," said Allen, a former architect-engineer. "I was asking myself, why don't they have better technology and actual data collectors?"[30]

---

[30] https://afrotech.com/this-blockchain-startup-allows-artists-to-collaborate-without-copyright-risks

As I've mentioned, I've had so many inspirations along my journey. Andrea Neiman shared her journey with me in a memorable way that would help define my entrepreneurial experience. Every encounter I've had with Andrea, who works for the CDC, is always positive. One day, she left me with some words of wisdom: "If you are not invited to the table, build your own." And that is exactly what I've set out to do, and I'm inviting you to do the same.

FUTURE WOMAN MINDSET: "If you are not invited to the table, build your own." —Andrea Neiman

Consortia

"By sharing information, collaborating organizations can keep their data up to date."

Blockchain technology requires a large number of players to be efficient. For that reason, various organizations, sometimes even competitors, have started to form alliances, known as consortia, that aim to create platforms used by every market participant in their sector. It's currently possible to observe such a trend in healthcare because blockchain can significantly increase interoperability and bring more efficiency while maintaining a high level of privacy and security. Both private and public entities are betting on collaboration to optimize their access to information.

Recently, IBM formed a partnership with Aetna, a health insurance giant, and other health insurers to build the Health Utility Network, a blockchain-based network. Their goal is to reduce cost in the healthcare industry by making claims more effective and improving the ways sensitive data is shared. Large amounts of money are inefficiently used in the healthcare system, and this impacts the profitability of organizations involved in this industry. Barbara Hayes, IBM general manager for payers at IBM Watson Health, told CoinDesk[31] that as much as 50 cents per dollar can be wastefully spent in the process.

So far, the partnership accounts for almost 100 million health plans and IBM expects additional members such as healthcare providers, technology companies, startups, and health organizations to join in the coming months. Among other things, the blockchain project encompasses a system for processing insurance claims and payments, which should decrease administrative costs and remove some duplication issues.

Synaptic Health Alliance is another consortium that's looking to improve the way partnering entities manage and share their data. According to their website, the seven founding members are Aetna, Ascension, Humana, MultiPlan, Optum, Quest Diagnostics, and UnitedHealthcare, all organizations that are currently impacted by inefficiencies plaguing the healthcare system.

Because insurers are legally required to maintain accurate data about physicians and other providers, each regulated organization ordinarily maintains a separate registry. However, the information is continuously changing, which leads the insurers to spend a lot of money and deploy considerable efforts to ensure that data is accurate. In April 2018, the consortium announced that they were launching a pilot program to see if blockchain could reduce administrative costs and improve data quality. By sharing information through a distributed ledger, they are hoping to make the ecosystem more efficient.

The pharmaceutical industry can benefit from blockchain because this

---

[31] https://www.coindesk.com/ibm-aetna-pnc-explore-medical-data-blockchain-for-100-million-health-plans

technology can be used to improve traceability within the drug supply chain. With a distributed ledger, both governmental bodies and private organizations could track medication distribution at different stages. Even though the U.S. Food and Drug Administration isn't currently using blockchain to conduct their activities, some recent developments revealed that the situation could evolve.

On February 7th, 2019, the FDA announced the launch of the Pilot Project Program under the Drug Supply Chain Security Act (DSCSA Pilot Project Program). This project will allow participants such as repackagers, manufacturers, and other stakeholders to trace and verify prescription drugs in the United States. According to their press release[32], the FDA is looking "to ensure suspect and illegitimate products do not enter the supply chain."

The organization also states that they're exploring new technologies that can improve the system, such as blockchain. The program is set to go into effect in 2023, and the FDA has hired Frank Yiannas, Walmart's former VP of Food Safety. Frank Yiannas has worked on the IBM Food Trust[33], one of the most successful supply-chain tracking systems powered by blockchain. Hence, the FDA may choose eventually to rely on a distributed ledger for some functionalities and processes.

Both public and private players are indubitably looking at blockchain as a potential means to improve communication between entities without neglecting security and privacy. Only time will tell if pilot

---

[32] https://www.fda.gov/news-events/press-announcements/fda-takes-new-steps-adopt-more-modern-technologies-improving-security-drug-supply-chain-through

[33] https://www.ibm.com/blockchain/solutions/food-trust

projects succeed in reducing structural costs, increasing access to information, and, therefore, improving profitability. While they explore these new opportunities, consortia need to avoid replicating situations where multiple groups are trapped within different silos. Healthcare has to be about patients' needs, which is why the entities involved have to cooperate to craft an efficient ecosystem.

In fact, Patientory wouldn't exist without the help and support of many other organizations. Patientory, Inc. was incorporated in late 2015 and initiated as part of the inaugural class of the Boomtown Health-Tech Accelerator in Boulder, Colorado in 2016. This led to a collaborative exchange with the Denver-based Colorado Permanente Medical Group, part of the Kaiser Permanente consortium, based in Oakland, California. Patientory is also part of the Startup Health portfolio, a global organization leading the movement to transform health. This led to the 2018 creation of the Patientory Association, a not-for-profit that connects healthcare industry adopters of the blockchain, the PTOYNetwork, and provides neutrality for its PTOY digital utility currency, which is utilized to provide users with access to the platform to store and secure health information.

PTOY generated enough buzz in the blockchain community that it managed to raise $7.2 million over a three-day period last year through cryptocurrency crowdfunding. The crowdfunding resulted in 1,728 contributors who bought 70 million PTOY utility-currency coins. The PTOY coins are utilized to access the PTOYNetwork, a private permissioned blockchain network with public data storage. Cryptocurrencies like bitcoin currently operate on similar blockchain.

This kind of consortia began with a question....*what if?*

Tools of the trade

"Women make up 51% of the U.S. population but less than 15% are financial advisors. They are drastically underrepresented in the financial advice industry and that makes it difficult for financial advice firms to meaningfully connect with this market. Often, women investors are treated as a niche market despite being a large demographic group with a range of perspectives, experiences, and interests."

— Marina Shtyrkov, research analyst,
wealth management with Boston-based Cerulli Associates.

Since I believe that financial empowerment is one of the keys that leads to transformation into the Future Woman mindset, I wanted to include a section here about where to go to learn, as I had to, about how to manage my money. I personally can't think of a bigger transformation than getting out of a mountain of debt or learning how to save hundreds of thousands of dollars while paying a mortgage.

While I was in the process of developing the skills I needed to take control of my finances, I wondered why they didn't teach these kinds of skills in school. When I talked to my friends about it, I remember hearing someone say something extreme about how colleges didn't like to talk about financial empowerment too much because then no one would take out student loans.

While there were always financial workshops around campus, I can't say why colleges seem to turn a blind eye to the practical management of money, or why students don't seek the knowledge out until they're in financial trouble. But what I can say about financial empowerment is that it begins with the everyday choices we make. I learned this through studying multiple experts on the subject of wealth and finance.

I'd like to take this section of the book to explore what female experts have to say about financial empowerment because their insight will help transform us to Future Women who take our financial skills to the next level.

FUTURE WOMAN MINDSET: You take on more career risk by staying put. (Sallie Krawcheck, Ellevest)

> *"You take on more career risk by staying put than if you actively push yourself in new directions. Failure is not game over. You get as many "at bats" as you choose to take...and let's face it, everyone loves a good comeback story."*
>
> —Sallie Krawcheck, CEO of Merrill Lynch, Smith Barney, U.S. Trust, the Citi Private Bank.

She was also Chief Financial Officer for Citigroup and a top research analyst covering the securities industry. Sallie knows a little bit about finance. She's often recognized as one of the most influential women in business. As CEO of Ellevest, a mission-driven investment platform for women; and Chair of a 135K global professional women's network called Ellevate Network, she's made it her mission to transform women's lives. She has a brilliant take on how women have been patronized in areas of finance from the time they're girls until they're older. Lots of times, they get the advice to not buy the latte and invest the money instead. I love her advice in an article, *Just Buy the f••ing latte.*

"All this nonsense about lattes and shoes is shifting the attention—and thus the blame—for the underlying systemic money challenges women face, to the women themselves. The pink tax, the wage gap, the debt gap, the funding gap, the domestic work (and emotional labor) gap, and—my personal crusade—the investing gap.

Don't look over there, where it says that the gender pay gap is decades away from closing for white women, 100-plus years away for Black women, 200-plus years for Latinx women: Let's focus on that the small luxuries you can give up. Don't pay attention to the fact that women carry a higher student loan burden than men do: Have you clipped your coupons? Let's not discuss that women are charged higher rates on loans and denied mortgages more frequently than men: Take this money quiz.

The fact that the U.S. is the only developed country in the world without a mandated paid maternity leave? The fact that just 15% of companies have a paid leave policy for their employees? The fact that 81% of women report having been sexually harassed? Well, those don't really fit the personal-guilt-being-sold-as-personal-empowerment narrative that sells so many books.

Women have effectively internalized the messages that our society sends them about money, and the result is that the primary emotion so many of us feel about money is shame. We feel shame when we are in debt; we feel shame because we spend too much, certainly; we feel shame because we earn too little–and we even feel shame because we earn too much. This is particularly so if women earn more than their male partners–which even today is a such a taboo that both parties will lie to the federal government about their incomes.

The result of this is that women prefer to talk about anything–literally anything–more than money, including their own deaths. At a time in which we openly speak about sex, money remains for women the final frontier of shame."

FUTURE WOMAN MINDSET: If you don't plan, you can't win. (Bola Sokunbi, Clever Girl Finance)

"For many people, budgeting is just not any fun. It means limits or lack of or even punishment. I personally prefer the word "plan" to the word "budget" because it doesn't sound so constraining. But having a budget in some form is really important for your financial success. Ever heard the saying "failing to plan is like planning to fail"? If you don't plan, you can't win."

—Bola Sokunbi, Clever Girl Finance

Bola Sokunbi's mission to help women become accountable, "ditch debt," and save with the goal of building wealth came because of how she lived in a family where her father took care of the money and her mother had little power as a result. This set her mother on the road to finding financial peace by going back to school and learning how to manage money and become a businesswoman, also known as the hustle queen. When the money ran out for her to go to college because of her father's forced early retirement, Bola's mom stepped in and paid for it in full. Afterwards, Bola saved her first $100,000 in just over 3 years with a starting salary of just $54,000 before taxes, even though she had a mortgage and other expenses.

FUTURE WOMAN MINDSET: Situations can change quickly. (Samantha Ealy, CEO, Generation Wealthy)

"It's really crazy how quickly situations can change when you've been working hard. Less than four years ago I was working three jobs, renting [a room in a] basement, living off ramen noodles, and spending what little free time I had studying for the GMAT. Fast forward to today — I work one amazing job, have a healthy diet, and I was recently accepted in Stanford's Graduate School of Business. All of my hard work from yesteryear has paid off." —Samantha Ealy

Her personal finance videos for teens and young adults will make sure that tomorrow's Future Women have a firm hold on finance as they take their first steps into the world of entrepreneurship.

Next level

The part I get excited about is building a movement to respond to something different than the old narratives. The days of our community coming together to raise awareness about the violence of minorities killed in the street aren't over, but we're going to change that narrative. We can build a proactive movement so that, for instance, when you go to school or learn a skill and you decide you want to be an entrepreneur for a high-growth technology company, we can see that your spirit isn't crushed because 500 people who called themselves investors tell you *no*. Instead, we can rely on one another and go to the party together to pool the financial resources we need to take our entrepreneurship to the next level.

If you want to talk about disruption, our communities have been "disrupted" far too long. I think opportunity lies in embracing technology and becoming knowledgeable about the science of the industry of blockchain and cryptocurrency. When you talk about the science of your industry, you feel really good about that, whether it's policy formation, social justice, economic justice, or education. I get excited about this because I can glimpse what the future can be for Future Women. If each one of us invested our black or brown dollars in our own entrepreneurs, what will the future hold?

Wealth leaves the community every time an outside investor invests on the Cap Table, which is basically the ledger of ownership. So we have to participate in the opportunity to invest early in minority companies. As Rodney Sampson, cofounder of Opportunity Hub, one of my advisors, and my copanelist on our panel *Talking Bitcoin, Blockchain, and cryptocurrency at Google World Headquarters in Silicon Valley,* said, "We are participating in our own demise by not making it a point to learn how to build each other up." Making money isn't dirty. The love of money may be, but making it and using it for the goal of uplifting our communities is essential to the creation of more Future Women.

As I've mentioned throughout the book, I've had many touchstones and many mentors, but I'll close this chapter on Transformation with a quote that I've kept with me that has helped me stay strong no matter what the tide:

"Have joy with our troubles because we know that these troubles produce patience and patience produces character and character produces hope."[34]

The gifts of staying persistent in transformation have been huge in my personal and professional life. In my personal life, I've been able to provide for my family and helped in part to send my younger sister to medical school by providing her a place to live.

She worked so hard to get to medical school. I needed to follow my passion, and it feels wonderful that I'm able to help her follow hers, a dream that we once shared. At times, it can feel impossible along the way to accomplishing your dream. However, I've found that when we're able to lift each other up during these times of trial, we contribute to making each other stronger while creating more Future Women.

FUTURE WOMAN MINDSET: Persist.

---

[34] Romans 5:3-4

EPILOGUE

"Little girls with dreams become women with vision."

—Chrissa McFarlane

I've always had a love of books. In fact, my 5th-grade teacher gave me "tokens" for reading stories that began my journey of empowerment, which would lead to my entrepreneurial journey into blockchain through a "token-ized" sale to create Patientory.

And it also led to hearing the tale of blockchain being a magical book. It wouldn't be fitting if your Future Women journey ended with this book. Rather, this is just the beginning. It's a call to action on the part of every female minority entrepreneur and everyone reading this book to clarify their dreams and visions.

As I wrote *FUTURE WOMEN: Minority Female Entrepreneurship and the Fourth Industrial Revolution in the Era of Blockchain and Cryptocurrency*, I began to see that I was a minority female entrepreneur championing a minority technology. In many ways, the battle I'm fighting for blockchain is similar to the battles I've had to fight in my own life as a female minority entrepreneur. I've had to battle prejudice and ignorance. I've had to educate and inform. And I've had to persevere with the kind of grit that I saw on the westerns my dad used to like to watch on the television when I was a little girl.

So, I'd like to add to the chain of Future Women who will link together to form the kind of strength we need to raise each other up as entrepreneurs and really build a foundation for the next Industrial Revolution and how it will reshape society.

Healthcare systems are cornerstones of all modern societies, since they provide vital services. As they grow, however, many become less efficient and secure, which can make healthcare services more expensive and less accessible to the general public. Beyond being the buzzword of 2017, blockchain opens the door to solutions in an increasing global healthcare expenditure that's expected to increase to USD 10.059 trillion by 2022.[35]

While the digitization of healthcare has paved the way for modern infrastructure, current privacy laws, software, and databases have slowly taken the power from the patient. Our existing software faces a few key problems that have both short-term and long-term implications, affecting both healthcare providers and their patients. Inefficiency, disjunction between databases, the disempowerment of patients, high expenses, and security concerns are just some of the many problems the healthcare industry faces.

Healthcare systems are remarkably inefficient. Since they operate with many independent databases, especially in large centralized systems, there's a lack of cohesive communication between these distinct silos. By creating a unified ecosystem of data, distributed ledger software encourages cooperation between networks, improving payment processing, patient tracking, and enterprise workflow.

Sectors like the food industry are already seeing wins with blockchain that healthcare can emulate in regards to supply chain management. Companies like Walmart implemented IBM's blockchain for food

---

[35] https://www2.deloitte.com/global/en/pages/life-sciences-and-healthcare/articles/global-health-care-sector-outlook.html

traceability, impacting pharmaceutical stakeholders to participate in the nonprofit Center for Supply Chain Studies DSCSA and Blockchain Phase 2 Study. The FDA who is behind this initiative, as declared by current FDA Commissioner Gottleib requires all entities governed under FDA "full implementation of the Drug Supply Chain Security Act[36], [and] to make sure that every link in the U.S. Drug Supply must be secure."

Other emerging use cases, such as clinical trials, involve the management of numerous locations, sources, and stakeholders, along with supervision of substantial amounts of sensitive data. Since blockchain may facilitate data storage, the technology can fuel innovation, as researchers will have greater access to medical record information.

The future of healthcare

Blockchain technology is expected to transform the way key players in healthcare systems interact with each other. Nonetheless, this technological revolution can only succeed with consortium thinking, which implies collaboration between all stakeholders in the sector. In the United States, Synaptic Health Alliance[37], a diverse consortium of healthcare organizations and other emerging startup consortia, are working to identify and monetize shared opportunities in the blockchain space.

But blockchain has problems. Right now, the initial costs can be high, and the integrations need to happen. Currently, most blockchain networks are designed so transactions are publicly accessible. While

---

[36] https://www.beckershospitalreview.com/supply-chain/blockchain-securing-the-healthcare-supply-chain.html

[37] https://www.synaptichealthalliance.com/

blockchain systems can be made private and permissible, making it so only certain parties can access boils down to aligned incentives. But it's clear that the technology is there and can change healthcare for the better.

"Disruptive"

According to a recent report put out by the Technology Association of Georgia in conjunction with the Georgia Institute of Technology[38], over twenty companies are devoted to blockchain in the metro Atlanta area. These include, BitPay, the largest bitcoin payment processor, and Storj and Patientory, which were the city's first two token sales. Several big corporations that call Atlanta home are also experimenting with blockchain; familiar names among others include Coca-Cola, State Farm, and UPS. Don Fortner, CEO of Valsurity and Ambassador to the Patientory Association, describes it as a "great step toward Atlanta becoming a Blockchain hub the same way it is a Fintech hub."

Fortunately, the concept of Atlanta becoming a blockchain mecca is inevitable. 70% of all global financial transactions[39] pass through companies headquartered in metro Atlanta. The city is dubbed as Transaction Alley, "due to the presence of payment processing leaders like First Data, WorldPay, Global Payments, and TSYS." New York and London may be global financial services leaders, but Atlanta is the unsung hero in global financial technology.

A large volume of financial transactions occurring in the city leads to

---

[38] https://www.docdroid.net/YnMFJjA/tag-blockchain-flash-report-2019f.pdf#page=4

[39] https://www.georgia.org/georgia-emerged-world-leader-fintech-due-presence-unprecedented-number-financial-technology-industry-leaders

large amounts of data and, of course, an increase in hackers, making it a priority for blockchain adoption. In the past two years alone, Atlanta experienced two of the largest data breaches to occur in history. The 2017 Equifax breach currently under litigation, cost over 400 million dollars, and the hackers extracted at least 146.6 million names, 146.6 million dates of birth, 145.5 million Social Security numbers, 99 million addresses, 17.6 million driver's license numbers, 209,000 credit card numbers, and 97,500 tax identification numbers. "This data breach is unprecedented. It affected almost half of the entire American population," notes U.S. District Judge Thomas W. Thrash.[40]

Then there was the Atlanta ransomware attack of 2018, which paralyzed the city for over a week, causing Mayor Keisha Lance Bottoms to take another look at the city's digital infrastructure.[41] "Just as much as we really focus on our physical infrastructure, we need to focus on the security of our digital infrastructure," Bottoms said. "I am looking forward to us really being a national model of how cities can shore themselves up and be stronger because of it."

We've had all kinds of new technologies enter into our lives and shape history, but I don't believe that any other technology has been called "disruptive." For example, back in the day, the railroads, airplanes, or electricity weren't seen this way either. They were technologies that were embraced.

It's a unique occurrence to view technological development that's revolutionary as "disruptive," especially one that has the potential to

---

[40] https://www.bizjournals.com/atlanta/news/2019/01/28/lawsuits-against-equifax-over-2017-data-breach.html

[41] https://www.cnn.com/2018/03/27/us/atlanta-ransomware-computers/index.html

really place power in the hands of the people. I think a lot of fear exists around blockchain because a lot of power is going to be taken away from centralized institutions. People who have the biggest stake in the financial status quo are framing the "disruptive" narrative.

I would like to disrupt the status quo in the world of female minority entrepreneurship. As part of my purpose and initiative to empower women, I established my Future Women small group through Victory World Church, my church home in Atlanta, a city that has become a center for aspiring young women who are looking to find their place in society.

Where are you on your journey? Have you been rejected, devalued, and marginalized? You're welcome in the pages of this book because *Future Women* will find a way to lift you up and take you out of that mindset and narrative and, instead, create a new story for you, one that finds you owning the abundant future that's your God-given right, that doesn't let other people or circumstances define you and, instead, hands you the keys to your entrepreneurial success.

APPENDIX:
THE PATIENTORY VISION

It's time to make healthcare personal

Our current health infrastructure has three inherent problems. Providers have to care for the growing number of over 117 million Americans diagnosed with a chronic health condition whose health information is distributed all over the place. On top of that, they're receiving fines for breach of patient information due to the absence of technology to safely secure protected health information (PHI). We need a secure, scalable, and cost-effective population health management solution that allows for interoperability—which just means how computer systems or software use and exchange information—and communication across different platforms when caring for a patient in order to receive the maximum improvement in care, especially for the chronically ill population.

Securing large amounts of data, scalability, and interoperability are all made possible with Patientory. Our system is an integrator. We have unique technology that enables us to seamlessly integrate with any electronic medical records (EMR) system, such as Meditech, EPIC, Allscripts, and Cerner. Through data and Artificial Intelligence (AI), our system is able to generate diagnoses and treatment plans as well as make predictions based on a population's data. In a nutshell, AI boils down to creating technology that thinks. So cloud applications adjust behaviors as you input your data as a user, so they "learn" about you in this way.

By seamlessly integrating with any electronic medical record, physicians or nurses can successfully treat a chronically ill patient by downloading medical information from the EMR and health wearable devices that are securely stored in blockchain servers to access and curate AI-powered care treatment plans. This system has the potential to eliminate the friction and costs of current third-party intermediaries when considering population health management.

Blockchain is a distributed data ledger and the recommended proven method for achieving minimal healthcare breaches. The care treatment plan is then made available directly to the patient's profile with automated required tasks. The clinician is able to stay in contact with the patient and their caregivers as well as track their treatment directives at home.

This promises improved data integrity, reduced transaction costs, decentralization, and disintermediation of trust. Being able to coordinate patient care via a blockchain Health Information Exchange (HIE) essentially alleviates unnecessary services and duplicate tests, which lowers costs and improves the efficiency of the continuum care cycle, while adhering to all HIPAA rules and standards. A patient-centered protocol supported by blockchain technology, Patientory is changing the way healthcare stakeholders manage electronic medical data and interact with clinical care teams.

In conjunction with health specific content, peer community, and family access, patient treatment directives are reinforced, improving health outcomes and decreasing hospital readmissions. The patient, in return, receives lifelong access to their information that can be shared with other providers, labs, and diagnostic services.

The business model is two-fold, incorporating consumers and

healthcare entities. Our annual recurring revenue comes from an annual SaaS fee and a one-time licensing and registration fee for healthcare entities. We also charge a medical information storage fee for users who exceed a certain amount of data, based on a Freemium plan. Last year, we laid the foundation for a global healthcare transformer as the leading solution for blockchain in healthcare. We received both national and global market validation and were named a Top 11 Company Disrupting Healthcare in 2017.[42]

We were also one of the first four companies in Colorado's first health-tech-specific accelerator and named a "Top 5 app empowering patients in the world" alongside products of multi-million-dollar companies.

We combine AI-powered population health management and cybersecurity to achieve results. Unlike other population health management solutions, which offer silo communities and rely on the actual user to manually input their information, Patientory strives to integrate all members involved in caring for a patient through an open healthcare network. Patients remain engaged through daily news and health tips enhanced by AI's ability to suggest peer-to-peer groups for patients to join.

We have an experienced team to accomplish our goals. In addition, I have a broad-based advisory board with expertise that spans healthcare and business, including Nigel Waller, who successfully exited his mobile device company to Blackberry in 2014.

So what is blockchain, anyway?

Blockchain is the technology behind the bitcoin digital currency.

[42] https://www.beckershospitalreview.com/hospital-management-administration/disruptive-healthcare-companies-to-watch-in-2017.html

Blockchain's birth is traced to the pseudonymous, unidentified person (or group) known as Satoshi Nakamoto. Since 2009, blockchain (think of it as software) has gained more widespread use in the finance industry with a variety of new blockchain-enabled businesses and services entering the market. Blockchain's technology is used to share a ledger of transactions across a business network without control by any single entity.

The distributed ledger makes it easier to create cost-efficient commercial relationships where virtually anything of value can be tracked and traded without requiring a central point of control (like a bank that charges fees, for example). The technology puts privacy and control of data in the hands of the individual. Trust and integrity are established without reliance on third-party intermediaries, like banks.

Distributed ledger technology

"A Brief History of Ledgers" by L. L. Fourn describes the interesting history of the ledger system:[43]

Hasib Anwar summarizes it nicely as follows:

> More than 5,000 years ago, clay tablets were used as a record keeping centralized ledger. Here, the ancient Mesopotamians would draw pictures in row and columns along with punching holes to keep track of how many items they had in store. Quite fascinating, isn't it?
>
> But about 700 years ago, a newer kind of centralized ledger system emerged in northern Italy. Here, merchants tried to accomplish a

---

[43] https://medium.com/unraveling-the-ouroboros/a-brief-history-of-ledgers-b6ab84a7ff41

logical connection between all the entries. Every item on the centralized ledger would have a debit and credit entry. So, you would have to enter the item twice. Apparently, this new form of the centralized ledger was the pathway to "capitalism."

The typical banking systems and keeping records came long after that. Where people used to keep everything recorded on paper. But after the invention of computers, everything started to digitize. In the 1980s and 90s computer systems started to take over the typical banking centralized ledger systems.

And just ten years ago, a new form of decentralized database structure emerged. In 2009, Satoshi Nakamoto introduced the first distributed ledger technology that gets rid of the whole authoritative environment and promotes a fairground.

And this is how the revolutionary decentralized ledger technology came into being.[44]

Distributed ledger systems began thousands of years ago, and that's really the technology that blockchain incorporates, only in a decentralized way. This is the perfect way to access and harness the power of the vast siloed personal healthcare data that exists for every individual and put it in their hands.

Current healthcare infrastructure

The realignment from a procedure-based focus to the holistic care of the individual requires care providers to form networks that work together toward a common goal of improving the health outcomes of patients under care for post-acute-care episodes or between acute-care

---

[44] https://101blockchains.com/distributed-ledger-technology-dlt/#1

episodes. The need for cooperation between care providers ranging from specialists, primary care physicians, caregivers, and wellness providers (like nutritionist and rehabilitation nurses) results in an increasing use of digital technologies. Though these solutions have significantly improved the tracking and efficiency for delivering care, they have resulted in creating silos of health information, primarily within electronic medical records (EMR) systems.

Healthcare and government organizations spend a significant amount of time and money setting up and managing traditional information systems and data exchanges, requiring resources to continuously troubleshoot issues, update field parameters, perform backup and recovery measures, and extract information for reporting purposes.

As a result, federal laws and incentive programs have made healthcare data more accessible in response to hospital pushback regarding EMR implementation. However, the vast majority of hospital systems still can't easily (or safely) share their data. As a result, doctors are spending more time typing than actually talking to patients. Physician burnouts jumped from 45% to 54% between 2011 and 2014.[45]

Although there exists the notion of "individualized" health information on both the clinical and wellness fronts, these haven't translated into "personalized" plans of care. Furthermore, even though a plethora of data exists, the overall healthcare ecosystem is incapable of adequately engineering a value or risk to big data to help better predict future care episodes of a patient.

Hence, the current solutions pursued by the healthcare technology

---

[45] "A Begoyan. An overview of interoperability standards for electronic health records." *Integrated Design and Process Technology* (2007).

industry have resulted in a difficult choice between care and privacy/economic concern for patients. At Patientory, we see this issue greatly expanding as more data is being created by the industry. Blockchain's secure technology, properties, and distributed nature can help reduce the cost and increase efficiency of these operations as well as provide a viable security infrastructure.

Patient-provider relationship

The new healthcare paradigm demands effective and optimal patient care delivery to yield better care outcomes. This requires that principal care providers are able to actively coordinate and collaborate with other care providers involved and ancillary health organizations such as labs and pharmacies. Ultimately, for this kind of coordination and collaboration to be successful, patient records need to be updated and modified promptly.

EMR software currently prohibits an effective patient-provider relationship. Current patient portals have minimal engagement among patients as a result of the siloed patient experience. Furthermore, this software solution only provides a limited capability to exchange information from one system to another and usually requires a designated individual capable of such information transfer. As a result, portals have led to an increasing amount of delay between organizations in delivering care for the patient and also resulted in an overall decrease in the quality and delivery of care services to the patient. Also, as care providers are spending more of their time involved in the coordination of care, their effectiveness in treating patients has decreased while their workload has significantly increased. This has resulted in a counterproductive impact on care outcomes for patients.

In addition, given that many doctors don't want patients to access

EHRs (Electronic Health Records), patients adopt a passive role in tracking their health. The current phenomenon around the lack of patient access to electronic medical information is a complex one. While many physicians believe patients don't need their data due to a lack of understanding of the information on file, the reality is this attitude puts the doctor at a higher risk of noncompliance and increased lawsuits. The controversial response from Judy Faulkner the Founder and CEO of Epic is telling. During an exchange between Joe Biden and Judy Faulkner, he asked her a question, "Why shouldn't patients have access to their medical records?" Her infamous response was "Why do you want your medical records? There are a thousand pages of which you understand 10."

The biggest issue in healthcare right now is regarding the legacy technologies that exist and the real cost and quality burden for healthcare at the moment because of the technology. With blockchain, we can see a bridge between a lot of the siloed information of medical records systems. Medical records were actually made to provide better treatment for the population, but it ended up being a capitalistic money grab where all these companies constructed what we call "walled gardens" because they don't want to share any information.

As a result, patients feel out of the loop concerning their own medical records and experience a lack of control and ownership of their health, which leads to patient frustration and, many times, disengaging from their care. Even though we have experienced a recent increase in mobile healthcare apps that help individuals track their vitals and health parameters, the novelty hasn't translated to improved patient care, adherence, or outcomes, as the apps also face the challenges of integration into EHRs.

System overview

Implementation of blockchain technology to ensure and enhance data security for all the medical records associated with the system can minimize health breaches and ultimately decentralize record ownership. The process of encrypting data when sent to a database using different algorithms and decrypting it during the retrieval will be used. Data shall be encrypted using NIST compliant algorithms during transmission and retrieval as is mandated by law. Thus, all exchange of information will comply with those best practices outlined in the NIST specifications. In view of the rapidly growing number of data breaches facing the healthcare industry, blockchain technology makes HIPAA compliance feasible for both patients and providers.

Blockchain system analysis of limitations due to HIPAA restrictions

The Ethereum Blockchain facilitates a diverse subset of system implementations due to the application of a Turing complete programming language that is executed on the Ethereum Virtual Machine. These systems have limitations in that the virtual machine has no direct outward-facing inspection of the broader Internet, except through the use of Oracle Services. Additionally, the storage limitations of the blockchain are enforced by the gas cost of storage and gas cost of access to this data. Gas is a unit denoting price of computation on the Ethereum, paid in Ether by users to miners in order to utilize the computational power of the network. A gas limit is the maximum amount of computational units that is allowed for your particular transaction.

As of this writing, the block time of the chain establishes a minimum bound for state modifying requests of at least fifteen seconds.

The limitation of the blockchain to host private information may be overcome through data obfuscation, such as encryption, but if the decryption key is ever leaked, vulnerabilities in accessing the information occur. For the purpose of HIPAA-compliant data, this may potentially result in a persistent, uncorrectable leak of information due to the immutability of the blockchain itself.

While the PTOYNetwork blockchain network uses a private permissioned flavor of the Ethereum Blockchain, it would be disastrous to assume that the deidentification filtering mechanism will never fail, or that the sideband information associated with blockchain interactions cannot inadvertently reveal identity without the proper network maintenance and consensus in place. This conclusion was also reached by the MIT Media Lab during the formation of the MedRec Protocols and summarized in the MedRec Whitepaper. Mining this sideband information may be as simple as observing timestamps and interactions with known data storage contracts.

Through this analysis, it may be possible to associate an individual with an institution and, more importantly, the time during which they were present at a facility. Given the specialized nature of some facilities, this is enough information to constitute a violation of HIPAA compliance due to a passive observer's ability to infer both identity, location, time of interaction, and, possibly, class of diagnosis.

Pending that this location is remote in nature, the reduction to less than 0.04% of the U.S. population becomes trivial. These facts constitute unreasonable single-point failures that must be acknowledged. Further, the direct storage of even encrypted information on the blockchain creates a responsibility of database managers to enter into a Business Associate Agreement due to their actions as a HIPAA data storage facility. This is an unreasonable expectation, since every miner and even those individuals hosting passive nodes would all need to be HIPAA compliant. Due to these concerns, we implement a mechanism for the persistent storage of sensitive information through private implementation of the Ethereum-based blockchain network.

Implementation goals for usability and security

The primary goals of any secure system may be summarized as the goals of confidentiality, integrity, availability, accountability, and information/identity assurance. In order to accommodate these goals, an attacker and user must be defined. Each of these roles demands certain acknowledgements of ability. From the perspective of the user, the system needs to be sufficiently transparent so that no advanced knowledge is needed. Also, due to the inability of the normal user to grasp the complex considerations of cybersecurity, the process needs to be resistant to the actions of the user.

If an attack occurs, the system is created such that the amount of effort that must be invested to compromise a resource is worth more than the value of the resource itself. This is due to the realization that a sufficiently advanced party with appropriate resources will always be capable of violating any system, given enough time and effort. More compactly, no perfect defense exists.

Definition of hardware and network implementation

To accommodate the above stated design goals, the selected system implementation requires several independent systems. Each system subdivides authority, ensures only authorized entities may interact in an approved manner, and provides a mechanism to increase security while maintaining availability. This system has also been devised such that scaling may be readily accomplished through the addition of hierarchical calling schemes.

The public-facing entity is a Remote Procedure Call (RPC) Server that acts as an interface to a private implementation of the Ethereum Blockchain (permissioned blockchain). This network of blockchain nodes (or blockchain storage network data sites for hosting protected health information), is only authorized to interact with the other blockchain nodes, a key authoring entity, the HIPAA-compliant storage facility, and the RPC Server. The key authoring entity is the resource that generates private/public key pairs for use on the blockchain. The HIPAA-compliant storage facility hosts the actual data that constitutes electronic private health information (ePHI).

When a request for data occurs, the HIPAA-compliant system may be authorized to speak to the forwarding agent, who then reroutes data back to the RPC server. Alternatively, it may be structured such that the HIPAA storage speaks directly to the RPC server. Each implementation has benefits that must be considered prior to final selection. In either event, the HIPAA storage facility decrypts the relevant portions of the database upon request handling. This decrypted information is then reencrypted, using the public key of the requesting party for transmission. This public key is also the public key of the contract that acts as the control interface from the blockchain to the HIPAA data.

Once a blockchain and its smart contracts are configured, the parameters become absolute. The patient becomes the primary intermediary in sending and receiving health information negating the need for frequent updates and troubleshooting of any software. Since blockchain records are also immutable and stored across all participating users, recovery contingencies are unnecessary. Moreover, blockchain's transparent information structure could abolish many data exchange integration points and time-consuming reporting activities.

Users are in control of all their information and transfers, which ensures high quality data that is complete, consistent, timely, accurate, and widely available, thus making it durable and reliable. Due to the decentralized database, blockchain does not have a central point of failure and is better able to withstand malicious attacks.

Any care network must ensure that participants who are collaborating together can depend on each other to deliver the necessary services that are expected of them. To achieve that, there has to be accountability of tasks and services and an expectation that they'll be delivered promptly. There also needs to be an associated liability if the services aren't promptly delivered at the level of quality that's expected. Hence, any healthcare infrastructure has to be able to seamlessly monitor the necessary information to enable the primary care provider to evaluate their care network. Furthermore, as the care network grows and these interactions between network care providers increase, the healthcare infrastructure should be capable of effectively scaling.

The key aspect to building a highly scalable and distributed care management system is a peer-to-peer framework. Such a framework has already been used in a number of industry segments such as media, sports, real estate, and supply-chain. Displaying blockchain can easily be an add-on software connector to existing centralized frameworks. This has led us to explore using the blockchain framework to help enable a peer-to-peer framework for healthcare.

Blockchain holds the promise of validating two or more entities engaged in a "healthcare transaction." This provides two key advantages compared to a centralized authentication model. The first being that interested parties can engage with each other at a "transaction level" of "trust relationship." The second that the liability exposure in such a relationship is limited to only "transaction-level" engagement. This is very useful, as it limits the access of information and liabilities between the parties involved and, at the same time, enables a party to get into a transaction relationship with a number of other providers based on their specific capabilities and type of care to be delivered to the patient. This is significantly better than conventional centralized systems needing to limit the number of providers for a wide range of patient needs.

Health Information Exchange and tokens

The Patientory token (PTOY) is the fuel for driving the blockchain infrastructure. The primary usage of the token is to regulate network storage allocation, healthcare quality measures, and revenue payment cycles. Patients are given an allotted amount of space to store information for free on the Patientory network. PTOY allows them to purchase extra storage space from nodes set up in hospitals systems. PTOY can be purchased via the platform or an exchange.

Healthcare organizations use PTOY in this instance as well. It is also used in payments once smart contracts are executed with healthcare insurance companies and serves as a mechanism to regulate value-based model metrics. In order for the United States to successfully move away from the fee-for-service model to the current value-based model, there has to be a healthcare IT infrastructure that allows organizations to link quality, value, and the effectiveness of medical interventions through a reputable compensation model.

Compensation will be based on how effective the network of providers work together to ensure improvement in the quality of care and wellness outcomes, while, at the same time, reducing associated care costs. To truly incentivize different participants in the network to proactively create better care regimes, a merit-based compensation of shared savings (reimbursements) takes effect. In order to effectively allocate a proportionate share to the provider in the network that contributed the most toward the overall savings, a clear tracking of their contribution is measurably executed by smart contracts on the blockchain network.

Another key impact of the new healthcare paradigm is the compensation model wherein providers are eligible for receiving additional compensation beyond the care delivered. This compensation is the result of savings that are generated based on how effectively the providers manage the care of the patient's health outcome (incentives). Any savings generated through efficient management of the patient's care can be retained by the providers and their network partners as part of the shared savings aspect of the new healthcare paradigm.

Patientory renders the ability for payors to transfer tokens as incentives to providers that achieve these quality metrics. The ability to seamlessly track and manage smart contracts in which the benefits can be redeemed with significant ease provides the necessary "carrot" for providers and patients to actively engage in a symbiotic collaboration. Contrarily, if one or more participants falters, appropriate penalties via liabilities, can also be levied with similar ease. This "carrot/stick" approach will provide the necessary push that's needed to shift the healthcare industry from a sickness management mindset to a wellness lifestyle mindset.

Henceforth, in exchange of PTOY tokens, users will be able to use the network to rent health information storage space, and to execute health specific smart contract payments and transactions.

We firmly believe that using a token is the best payment system to support this infrastructure for the foreseeable future. The future is a vibrant ecosystem of many tokens, for which healthcare will need a closed loop payment system in place. The result will be an efficient care cycle management positive feedback loop with significant decreases in billions of dollars currently attributed to healthcare payment fraud.[46]

The system also issues incentives to those large organizations with ample server storage to trade tokens with small- to medium-sized healthcare organizations that will need direct access into the blockchain health network without directly implementing a node. Though the new healthcare policies provide the potential to incentivize providers to work together to improve care pathways, the current EHR architectures fall short of enabling this ability; thus, simply granting or receiving tokens facilitates this process.

Therefore, tokens are tied to the volume of transactions executed in the network. As the Patientory network consistently increases in token transactions, the demand for the token increases. PTOY can be acquired through Patientory's native app, cryptocurrency markets, and from another patient, physician, or insurer via transfer.

Additional unique benefits

Although a medical institution, such as a hospital, should not have access to any records that haven't been specifically approved, by having

---

[46] National Healthcare Anti-Fraud Association. "The Challenge of Health Care Fraud." In: https://www.nhcaa.org/resources/health-care-anti-fraud-resources/the-challenge-of-health-care-fraud.aspx.

users preauthorize the sharing of information under emergency circumstances, the end user could derive additional benefit from participation in the service. With this in mind, the need of a medical facility to access the records of an unresponsive person in an emergency constitutes a situation that merits privilege escalation, given the user has previously authorized this access.

If a person is unresponsive and has their cell phone present, the institution may access it by using a secondary signature method that's available from the lock screen of a smartphone. This second key must not be the same private key as the primary account. Thus, if an institution account submits a request to the blockchain containing the public key of an individual and the smartphone of that individual has submitted an emergency signature, the blockchain may escalate privilege to allow access to medical records it would not otherwise have access to. This private key should be considered disposable and be replaced by the individual as soon as possible. In this manner, the secure exchange of information between an individual and an authorized institution may be facilitated in emergency conditions.

Should an institution request this information without appropriate authorization, the individual would be notified of the actions. If the individual denies this request within a threshold interval, the data isn't shared. Further, if an institution attempts multiple fraudulent requests, the institution may be punished by revocation of privilege, fines, and/or legal actions. The damage caused by losing a cellular device is minimal due to the need for both a cellular device and an institution-level key. In the foreseeable future, all insurance cards could be embedded with cryptographic microcontrollers, just like modern credit cards possess, that would facilitate the same operation independent of a smartphone.

National/International healthcare priorities

Personalized care. To achieve effective superior care, a person-centric approach is important. Such an approach should consider not only the clinical aspects but also the social and economic factors that impede one's ability to successfully engage in care compliance and healthy living to yield sustained wellness.

To yield effective care outcomes requires clearly identifying the barriers of individual health and life situations. With the growing number of patients having two or more comorbidities, the "siloed" one-size-fits-all care delivery approach isn't conducive in motivating and addressing effective care outcomes. Hence, a more flexible care model tailored to include patients' multifaceted health and wellness needs has to be considered. This requires a comprehensive, dynamic interactive care plan that the patient can actively track and manage.

Clinical outcomes. Patient-related outcome measures (PROMs), which focus on outcomes that are directly related to the patient, have taken on added importance and significance over the past several years. This is due, in part, to the increased attention focused on the patient experience of care and to provide a patient-focused assessment on the burden and impact of disease. PROMs can include symptoms and other aspects of health–related quality of life indicators such as physical or social function, treatment adherence, and satisfaction with treatment. They can also facilitate more accurate patient-physician communication in terms of the burden of treatment-related morbidities by providing a more detailed and complete evaluation of treatments for specific conditions, such as cancer or multiple sclerosis.

PROMs are distinct from traditional clinical efficacy measures (e.g., survival in cancer, smoking cessation) because they directly reflect the impact of disease and its treatment from the patient's perspective. These measures can examine the balance between the efficiency of the treatment and its burden on the patient. It's also effective in looking at areas such as physical functioning and overall well-being, and highlighting the efficacy and safety of a treatment in relation to its overall clinical benefit. Because the measures themselves are developed from the patient's perspective, it can also facilitate greater patient involvement in treatment decision making as well as providing guidance for healthcare decisions. Essentially, reinforcing a blockchain PROM infrastructure reinforces the ability to incentivize providers and payors in meeting care standards.

Entrepreneurial challenges

On the outside, entrepreneurship looks glamorous, yet, at its core, lies hard work, day-in and day-out, like a mechanic building a Ferrari. I focused on cultivating and keeping relationships—they are the key. My vision for Patientory had to be laid out in a way that key stakeholders could understand. Much of the information had to be put into a white paper that was distributed to potential supporters of the concept. This resulted in our token acquisition round which occurred on a crowdfunding website. When all was said and done, we had a $7.2-million first round of Ethereum-based PTOY tokens raised to create the blockchain network.

Patientory, Inc. also launched a $5.2 million Series A round of funding, which included R/GA Ventures. This marked the first funding round since we split from the Patientory nonprofit created after the 2017 token sale of $7.2 million. Patientory, Inc. was chosen for the recent round of funding because of the meaningful way that I managed our token sale funds through a bear market. The new Series A round will go toward developing more features for our mobile app. Since our launch in 2018, nearly 350 users have tested our beta mobile app, which can include subscription features like personalized health tips.

To date, the Patientory ecosystem has raised close to $12.4 million from the token sale to the latest venture capital round. Beyond the holdings given to the founding team and nonprofit, few people are trading PTOY tokens currently on external exchanges like Upbit and Bittrex. While the price of PTOY has taken a hit in the bear market, Patientory also accepts fiat payments from prospective clients and then purchases tokens on their behalf to facilitate transactions. The crypto bear market of 2018 is longest on record, going on 2 years, and a halving event likely to occur in May 2020 will change the bitcoin price forever. Node operators can earn PTOY tokens as a reward for providing storage space to other network participants, but we don't make the usage of our tokens mandatory.

About a third of the token sale funds went toward the nonprofit's marketing and conference budget and nonprofit management, including recruiting and participating in our Dubai's BlockHealth Summit in the spring of 2019. Another 20% went toward developing our app, which enabled us to keep seven developers on staff. The remaining 45% of the token sale funds are under the nonprofit's management, predominantly ether reserves along with 5% in conservative, traditional investment products. Most of the token sale funds went to establishing the nonprofit—three board members, four institutional members and a dozen ambassadors promoting the blockchain solution abroad.

BlockInterop CEO Gina Malak, is a PTOY holder who plans to run a node (blockchain storage network data site for hosting protected health information) pay for Patientory's blockchain-as-service offerings and collaborate on workshops through the Patientory Association. It's been refreshing working with Gina, as we're both Black female entrepreneurs who needed to explore token sales to finance our companies because of the staggering statistics against traditional venture capital funding for Black women.

Today, Patientory has a slowly growing community of contributors and association members involved with focus groups to figure out the best compliant solutions for sharing sensitive healthcare data. We're currently participating in an OEBVS program to explore research opportunities with partners and have ongoing pilot programs with partners that run their own nodes, including Moda Health and IrisGuard, the latter credited with running an aid distribution program with the United Nations in 2017 to serve refugees in Jordan. Patientory is also pursuing opportunities with the Dubai Health Authority. I feel that, together with partners, we have formed a strong strategic alliance that will empower patients and bring them to the center of their healthcare.

ACKNOWLEDGMENTS

Thank you to the following who helped make this book possible:

Boomtown Healthtech Accelerator

RGA Ventures

Atlanta Tech Village

Startup Health

Women's Startup Lab

Advisors:

Rodney Sampson

Nigel Waller

Kirk Barnes

Frenesa Hall, MD

Shawn Wilkinson

Peter Kung

Rick Brounstein

Richard DiMonda

Geetha Rao

RESOURCES

Future Women Mindsets

Minority & Mindset

- Show value in transformational ways people have never seen before.
- If you don't know it, learn it.
- Nurture and protect your mindset like a little baby. Give it good care and feeding.
- Let struggles strengthen your opportunities so you grow through challenges.
- Always move forward.
- Do everything you can do to master everything that is under your control.
- Common sense isn't sold in a shop.

Flexibility

- Consider your Version 1.0 and version 2.0.
- Follow your heart and intuition.
- Stay open to opportunities that you don't expect.
- Have faith in yourself and your dream.
- Take care of your body, mind and spirit every day.
- When you need help, ask for it.
- Future Women need each other, cultivate a generosity of spirit together.

Financial Empowerment

- Be in control of your finances instead of having your finances dictate the choices you have to make in life.

- Prioritize seeking and finding the right opportunity, and become clear about financial objectives.

- Financial empowerment leads to financial freedom, which allows people more flexibility in their lifestyle and work-life balance.

- Financial empowerment leads to empowering others on their journey.

- Future Women give back and pay it forward.

- Financial empowerment allows you to dream big.

- You are the creator of your own experience including what kind of opportunities you want to create and where you want to have those experiences.

- Having resources at key times in my life proved useful in the formation of my career.

- Being a good steward of your money involves the planning process.

- The acceptance of where you are now, instead of beating yourself up over it, allows for you to recognize and take advantage of opportunities that would certainly pass you by otherwise.

- Comparison doesn't serve us. Breaking the mold does.

- Have advisors who have a heart for helping to build your company the way you imagine.

- Stay flexible and seek out new connections that open up ways you might not have originally considered.

Inspiration

- Stay true to yourself.
- Sometimes, when you're down or experiencing a lot of resistance, you close off. I've found it's important to do the opposite. Don't miss the rainbow after the rain.
- Take the judgement out of your experience since labels are never helpful.
- Instead of arguing about the current state of affairs, we need to change the narrative.
- Don't take anything personally.
- Fill the gaps with entrepreneurial companies.
- Don't let cautionary tales frame the narrative.
- Dream boldly about the future.
- Go where the spirit leads.
- Hold to your values and beliefs.
- Build on your intelligence and influence to lift up other female entrepreneurs.
- Know your why.

Transformation

- Opportunity lies just beyond those "closed doors."
- Be comfortable with the uncomfortable and challenge yourself to go outside your comfort zone.
- Share their perspectives and help give real-world information to other women in order to help shape their careers.
- "If you are not invited to the table, build your own." — Andrea Neiman
- You take on more career risk by staying put.
- If you don't plan, you can't win.

- Situations can change quickly.
- Persist.

Books and References

The Five Dysfunctions of a Team, by Patrick Lencioni

The Alchemist, by Paulo Coelho

Think and Grow Rich! by Napoleon Hill

Bad Blood: Secrets and Lies in a Silicon Valley Startup, by John Carreyrou

Engage!: Transforming Healthcare Through Digital Patient Engagement (HIMSS Book Series), by Jan Oldenburg, Dave Chase, Kate T. Christensen, and Brad Tritle (Eds.).

Bitcoin: A Peer-to-Peer Electronic Cash System, by Satoshi Nakamoto.

Links

https://patientory.com/

https://ehealthradio.podbean.com/e/blockchain-in-healthcare-with-chrissa-mcfarlane

http://newtrusteconomy.com/healthcare-blockchain-with-chrissa-mcfarlane

https://hitlikeagirlpod.com/chrissa-mcfarlane/

Organizations

The Frontrunners League, and Blockchain Ladies: The Network

www.ingramcontent.com/pod-product-compliance
Lightning Source LLC
Chambersburg PA
CBHW050459190326
41458CB00005B/1356

9 781950 336128